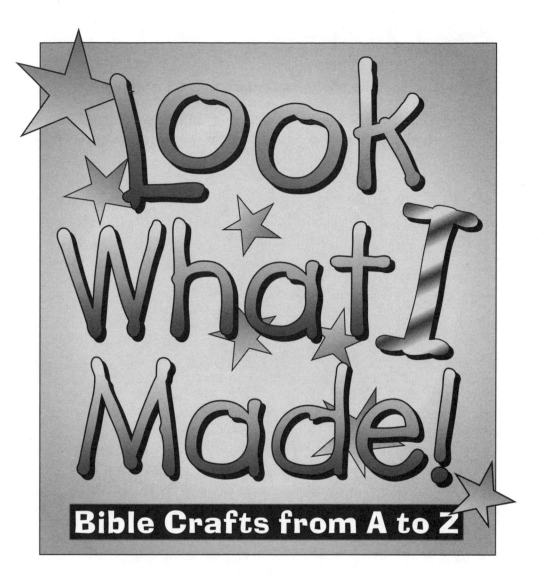

Look What I Made!

Bible Crafts from A to Z

by Anita Reith Stohs

CONCORDIA PUBLISHING HOUSE · SAINT LOUIS

To Matthew, Miriam, and Christopher

*We are God's workmanship, created in Christ Jesus to do good works,
which God prepared in advance for us to do. Ephesians 2:10*

Editor: Cynthia A. Wheeler
Editorial Assistant: Marlene Maxfield

Scripture taken from the HOLY BIBLE, NEW INTERNATIONAL VERSION®. Copyright © 1973, 1978, 1984 by
International Bible Society. Used by permission of Zondervan Publishing House. All rights reserved.

Copyright © 1998 by Concordia Publishing House
3558 S. Jefferson Avenue, St. Louis MO 63118-3968
Manufactured in the United States of America

06   07   08   09   10   11   10   09   08   07   06   05

Contents

Look What I Made!

"Look what I made!" Can you hear the child's proud words as he pushes his newest creation into your hands? Can you see her joyful expression as she shows you her work? This book is filled with a multitude of look-what-I-made crafts that will delight and challenge children. Each craft is made from a familiar item to make Bible crafts that echo or reinforce Bible stories of themes. You can also use the ideas to make your own effective Bible story teaching materials.

Creativity is a gift of God, who made the world with infinite variety. These activities will draw you into the God-given creative process and launch you into your own craft discoveries. Adapt projects to use the materials on hand. Always look beyond the visual impact of the project for the way it can enhance the purpose of the Bible lesson it accompanies.

Let your students explore their own unique shoots and sprouts of creativity. Active involvement with arts and crafts can provide a greater understanding of a Bible lesson or theme. Talk together as you work. Ask questions about the Bible lesson. Discuss how the activity reviews the Bible story or reinforces a truth in the children's lives. This discussion will help children extend learning from their heads to their hearts and hands.

Anita Reith Stohs

apple

Bible Apple Doll

Supplies ...
- Apple
- Paring knife
- Plastic knife and spoon
- Craft stick
- Yarn
- Fabric scraps
- Glue

Directions ...
Have an adult use the paring knife to peel the apple. Use the plastic utensils to cut a rough face out of the peeled apple. Let the apple shrivel and dry for a week. Then insert a craft stick into the bottom of the apple. Remove the stick; put glue in the hole; re-insert the stick. Cut and glue clothes to the stick. Add yarn hair. Use the doll in a display or as a puppet.

Options and Variations ...
❶ Use cotton or craft hair instead of yarn.
❷ Add chenille-wire arms.

The Lesson Connection ...
God keeps His promises to Abraham (Genesis 12:1–25:11)
Make an Abraham puppet to tell the story of his life. Cut a fabric headdress and tunic. Add a yarn belt and headband. Add cotton as a beard.

John is born (Luke 1:57–80)
Make Zechariah and Elizabeth characters. Wrap a peanut in fabric to represent baby John.

★★★★★★★★★★★ applesauce

Ornament

Directions ...

Make dough from 2 parts applesauce, 1 part cinnamon, 1 part flour. Mix cinnamon and flour, add applesauce until the dough is stiff. Roll dough to ¼″ thickness. Do not add more flour. Cut out a shape with a cookie cutter or knife. Punch a hole with a pen at the top. Dry on a rack, turning twice a day until dry (about 2 days). Tie a ribbon thru the hole for a hanger.

Options and Variations ...

❶ Bake at 225° for about 2 hours.
❷ Incise or stamp designs into the dough.
❸ Combine shapes to make larger ornaments.
❹ Paint designs on dried ornaments with fabric paint.

The Lesson Connection ...

God helps Joseph forgive his brothers (Genesis 42–45)
Make a heart-shaped ornament. Stamp designs on the edge or center, or cut a 2nd heart out of the center.

An angel visits Mary (Luke 1:26–55)
Cut out an angel with a Christmas cookie cutter. Hang the finished ornament on your Christmas tree.

Supplies ...

- Applesauce
- Cinnamon
- Flour
- Measuring cup
- Mixing bowl and spoon
- Rolling pin
- Knife or cookie cutters
- Pen
- Cookie rack
- Ribbon

bread

Christian Witness Jewelry

Supplies ...
- White bread
- White glue
- Food coloring
- Ziplock bag
- Rolling pin
- Cookie cutters
- Pencil
- Acrylic sealer
- Safety pin, cord, or ribbon

Directions ...
In a ziplock bag, mix together bread and glue (1 tablespoon of glue for each slice of bread). Add food coloring. Knead together for 8–10 minutes until smooth, pliable, and uniform in color. The dough will be sticky, but will change when kneaded. Add flour or water if the dough is too sticky or stiff. Roll out the dough. Cut out shapes. To make a medallion, poke a hole in the top with a pencil. To make a pin, push the pin into the wet dough; let dry. Paint with acrylic sealer. String the medallion on cord or ribbon to wear.

Options and Variations ...
❶ Decorate with sequins or other trims.
❷ Glue magnetic strips to the back of the shapes to make refrigerator magnets.
❸ Mold dough into 3-D shapes by hand.
❹ Stick dough to a porous surface when wet or glue to a nonporous surface when dry.
❺ Substitute tacky glue for a porcelain-look finish.

The Lesson Connection ...
God helps Joseph forgive his brothers (Genesis 42–45)
Stick a small heart onto a larger heart. Tell the students that God sent Jesus to die on the cross for our sin because He loves us. He forgives us and helps us forgive others.

Jesus calls His disciples (Mark 1:14–20; John 1:35–51)
Cut out a foot shape. Draw a cross on it. Punch a hole at the top and add a shoestring to make a necklace. Remind students to "Follow Jesus" in all they say and do.

★★★★★★★★★ bulletin picture

Bible Verse Gift Box

Directions ...

Fold 1 corner of the bulletin picture over to the other edge. The folded piece will look like a triangle. Score this and all folds with a pencil. Cut away the extra paper (*fig. 1*). Unfold. Fold the square into quarters (*fig. 2*), picture side out. Unfold. The paper will look like figure 3. Now fold each corner to the center (*fig. 4*). Fold each side over about 1", or the depth you want the box (*fig. 5*). Gently unfold. Now fold the small square corners to the inside (*fig. 6*). Glue or tape. To make a lid, cut a square about ¼" larger than the original bulletin picture and repeat the directions. Cut strips of colored paper. Write your favorite Bible verses on them and put them inside the box. Tie the box with ribbon.

Options and Variations ...

❶ Use the box to store Bible verses learned during a course of study.
❷ Make boxes from calendars, magazines, or wrapping paper.
❸ Write on the box with a metallic marker.
❹ Make larger boxes to hold other gift items.

The Lesson Connection ...

David praises God (Psalms)
Write favorite Psalms verses to fit inside the box.

Philip witnesses to an Ethiopian (Acts 8:26–40)
Write Bible verses that tell that Jesus is God's gift to us (e.g., Romans 6:23; Ephesians 2:8–10).

Supplies ...

- Bulletin picture
- Scissors
- Pencil
- Glue or tape
- Colored paper
- Fine-tipped markers
- Ribbon

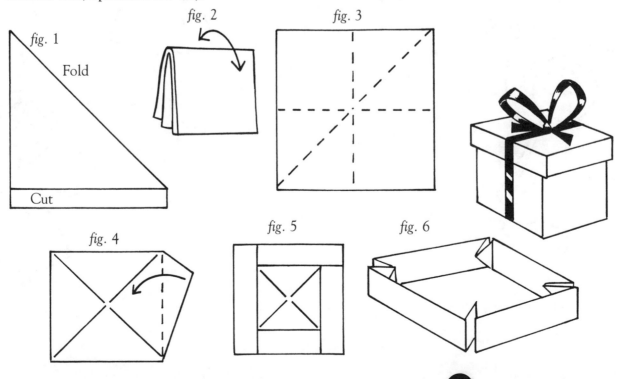

fig. 1 Fold Cut

fig. 2

fig. 3

fig. 4

fig. 5

fig. 6

★★★★★★★★ candy sucker

Stick Puppet

Directions ...
Place a napkin over the top of a candy sucker. Twist the napkin and tie yarn at the top of the stick to make a puppet head. Cut another napkin in half; fit it around the candy for a headdress. Glue down. Tie on a piece of yarn as a headband. Cut and fray small pieces of yarn; glue them on as hair and beards.

Options and Variations ...
❶ Substitute colored tissue paper or fabric for napkins.
❷ Draw a face on a round, gummed label. Stick to the sucker.
❸ Cut a 2nd napkin as a tunic. Fold in half, cut a hole for the head, and place on the sucker. Tie a yarn waistband.
❹ Add chenille-wire arms.
❺ Follow directions for washcloth puppets found on page 101 of this book.

The Lesson Connection ...
David and Jonathan (1 Samuel 17:55–20:42)
Have each child make 2 puppets—David and Jonathan. Use them to review the story.

An angel visits Mary (Luke 1:26–55)
Make an angel to tell different parts of the Christmas story from an angel's point of view. Add metallic chenille-wire wings and halo.

Supplies ...
• Candy sucker
• Paper napkins
• Yarn
• Glue
• Scissors

canning lid ★★★★★★★★★★★★

Wall Hanging

Supplies ...

- Canning lid
- Acrylic paint
- Paintbrush and water
- Lace
- Metallic cord
- Scissors
- Tacky craft glue

Directions ...

Paint a Christian symbol or word onto the lid. Cut and glue a strip of lace around the edge on the backside of the lid. Glue a loop of metallic cord to the back of the lid.

Options and Variations ...

❶ Glue fabric over the lid; glue on dried or artificial flowers.
❷ Glue on a picture cut from a leaflet or card.
❸ Substitute a frozen fruit juice lid for the canning lid.
❹ Have older children sketch a design with a pencil, then poke holes with a hammer and nails to outline it.

The Lesson Connection ...

Fruit of the Spirit (Galatians 5:22–23)
Make a symbol for each fruit on separate lids. Hang them on a strip of fabric or ribbon. Attach a pop-top tab to the back for a hanger.

Jesus loves me (Galatians 2:20b)
Read the Bible verse together—" I live by faith in the Son of God, who loved me and gave Himself for me." Draw a picture or symbol that tells about the verse.

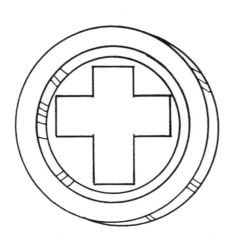
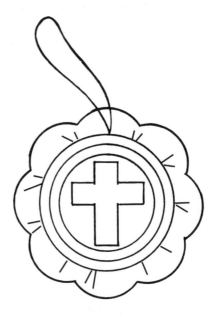

cardboard

Stand-Up Figure

Directions ...

Draw a Bible figure on a piece of paper. Glue the figure to cardboard, then color it and cut it out, leaving a rectangular base around the feet. To stand the figure up, cut a slit in the base. Fold 1 part forward and the other part backwards.

Options and Variations ...

❶ For more stability, glue a cardboard triangle or circle to the back of the figure.

❷ Use figures from student leaflets to make Bible people. Cut figures from catalogs or magazines to make contemporary puppets.

❸ Make life-sized, stand-up figures of your students.

❹ Make stand-up scenery to go with the figures.

The Lesson Connection ...

God gives victory thru judges (Judges 4; 6–7; 13–16)
Have the students make stand-up models of Israelite judges (e.g., Deborah, Gideon, and Samson), then tell about them.

Jesus calls His disciples (Mark 1:14–20; John 1:35–51)
Make stand-up figures of Jesus and all the children in the class.

Supplies ...

• Paper
• Cardboard
• Markers or crayons
• Scissors

cardboard box ★★★★★★★★★★

Play Church

Supplies ...

- Cardboard box
- Sharp scissors or knife
- Markers or crayons

Directions ...

Draw a general outline of a church on the box. Have an adult cut out or hinge the top, windows, and the front door. Cut the end flaps to make a triangle. Tape the ends to the side panels to make a roof. Make a cross from cardboard scraps and add it to the top. Draw in details.

Options and Variations ...

❶ Add color with paint, adhesive-backed paper, and/or fabric.
❷ Make a replica of your own church or design a new one.
❸ Make a Bible-time house from a carton.

The Lesson Connection ...

Solomon builds the temple (1 Kings 5–8)
Make a model of the temple. Act out Bible stories that take place there.

The boy Jesus visits the temple (Luke 2:41–52)
Construct a model of your church. Use it to teach the children how to participate in worship.

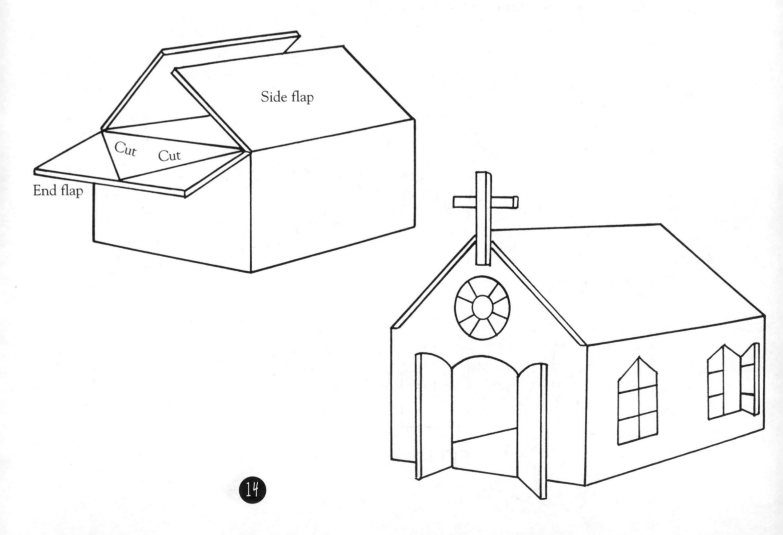

⭐⭐⭐⭐⭐⭐⭐ cardboard tube

Palm Tree

Directions ...

Rescue a large cardboard tube from a carpet store (from inside carpet or vinyl rolls) or make a tube by taping oatmeal boxes together. Cut open the paper bags. Cut off the bottoms. Cut 8–10″ wide strips. Cut fringe along 1 long side. (Layer bags to fringe more than 1 at a time.) Start at the top of the tube and glue these paper-bag strips around the tube with fringe pointing up. Cut leaf shapes out of green construction paper. Fringe the edges. Glue into the top of the tube.

Options and Variations ...

❶ Use many trees to make a jungle corner in your room for quiet reading or games.

❷ Encourage students to personalize their trees with messages "carved" into the "bark."

❸ Make coconuts from wadded-up newspaper. Paint with brown paint. Or stuff small paper bags with newspaper. Form into balls and attach to trees with tape.

The Lesson Connection ...

Jesus enters Jerusalem—Palm Sunday (Matthew 21:1–11)
Make palm trees to line an imaginary road to Jerusalem. Make extra palm leaves for students to use as you act out or tell the story of Palm Sunday.

Supplies ...

• Cardboard tube
• Brown paper bags
• Scissors
• Green construction paper
• Glue

cereal box ☆☆☆☆☆☆☆☆☆☆

Mini-Puppet Stage

Supplies ...

- Cereal box
- Cardboard or poster board
- Paper
- Scissors
- Glue
- Markers, crayons, or colored pencils

Directions ...

Have an adult cut a stage opening in the front of the box. Cover the outside and inside with paper. Glue paper curtains around the stage. Cut vertical slits in the top and bottom of the sides of the box. Cut a cardboard strip long enough to slide thru the slits. Draw and color a Bible character, then cut it out. Glue cardboard support to the back, then glue the figure to the cardboard strip. Move the strip back and forth as you tell the story.

Options and Variations ...

❶ Cut additional slits for more characters, or add several figures to the same strip.

❷ Glue on fabric curtains. Cover the box with wrapping or adhesive-backed paper.

❸ Draw different background scenes to glue behind the stage opening or attach to a separate cardboard strip.

❹ Cut out figures from old leaflets or magazines to use as puppets.

❺ Have stage creators share their Bible story with younger children.

The Lesson Connection ...

Crossing the Red Sea (Exodus 13:17–15:21)

Prepare 3 strips to illustrate sky, water, and the sandy bottom of the Red Sea. Draw a wall of water as the background scene of the stage. Draw and glue a row of people to another strip. Start the story with the sky and water strips in front. Pull the water strip out to reveal the sand strip. Pull the people strip to show God's people safely walking thru the water.

The good Samaritan (Luke 10:25–37)

Cut 2 strips. On 1, glue a figure of the injured man. On the other, glue the Levite, priest, and Samaritan figures. Pull the strip with the 3 men as you tell how each responded to the injured man. Pull the strip with the injured man to show how the Samaritan carried him to safety.

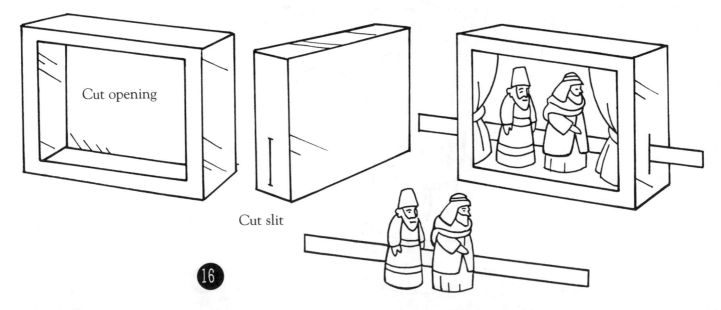

Cut opening

Cut slit

✦✦✦✦✦✦✦✦✦✦ clothespins

Stand-Up Figures

Directions ...

To make Bible people: Twist chenille wire around a clothespin to make arms. Draw facial features. Glue on movable eyes. To make a robe, fold a rectangular piece of felt in half and cut a hole in the fold for the head. Pull the felt over the top of the clothespin. Tie a piece of yarn as a belt. Fray yarn ends to make hair or a beard. Glue in place. Use felt or chenille wires to add other details. Stand the figure in a ball of oil-based clay.

To make a donkey: Turn 1 clothespin upside down as the head and ears. Stand 2 clothespins right side up to be legs. Glue the pieces together with wood glue. As an option, connect the leg pieces with a craft stick or coiled chenille wire. Paint the clothespins brown. Glue on movable eyes and a frayed yarn mane.

Options and Variations ...

❶ Place a cotton or Styrofoam ball on the top of a clothespin to make a head. Cover it with a square cut from panty hose material. Tie in place with a string or piece of yarn.

❷ Omit fabric. Color all features with markers.

❸ Make a cardboard-box stage.

The Lesson Connection ...

Balaam blesses Israel (Numbers 22–24)
Make figures for Balaam, his donkey, and the angel of the Lord.

Jesus' family escapes to Egypt (Matthew 2:13–23)
Make figures for Mary, Joseph, Jesus, and the donkey. (Cut off the top of a clothespin to represent the 2-year-old Jesus.)

Supplies ...

- Peg clothespins
- Chenille wires
- Movable eyes
- Felt
- Scissors
- Glue
- Yarn
- Fine-point markers
- Oil-based modeling clay

Additional materials for donkey:
- Wood glue
- Acrylic paint and brush

Fold

Cut

construction paper ★ ★ ★ ★ ★ ★

Storytelling Tube

Supplies ...

- Construction paper
- Long piece of paper
- Pencil
- Scissors
- Markers
- Glue

Directions ...

Define major scenes of a story and divide the long piece of paper into a section for each. Draw or cut and glue shapes to the paper to complete the scenes. Glue the edges of the paper together to make a tube that stands up. For easier turning, glue the tube to a cardboard circle or paper plate. Turn the tube to tell the story.

Options and Variations ...

❶ Place objects (e.g., model boat, stand-up figures) in front.
❷ Cover a large oatmeal box to make the tube.
❸ Make a storytelling cone instead of a tube.
❹ Decorate the tube with stickers or cut-out pictures.
❺ Have tube creators share their Bible story with other children.

The Lesson Connection ...

God made the world (Genesis 1:1–2:3)
Divide the paper into 6 sections to illustrate the 6 days of creation. Add these words: "God made all things well."

Kings worship Jesus (Matthew 2:1–12)
Cut a tube from dark-blue paper. Cut and glue a yellow "desert" strip around the bottom. Add metallic star stickers. Add Bethlehem buildings with a larger star above. Cut out a drawing of the 3 Wise Men, leaving a strip at the bottom. Slit the strip. Fold 1 strip forward and the other backwards. Stand up the Wise Men in front of the tube. Turn the tube to show them traveling.

cork

Model House

Directions ...
Rinse out a milk carton and let dry. Trace the 6 sides of the carton (ends, top, and sides) onto the cork. (Trace the 2 roof pieces about 1" longer than the carton.) Cut out the pieces; glue them to the carton. Decorate with markers.

Options and Variations ...
❶ Decorate with acrylic paint, paint pens, or fabric paint.
❷ Glue photographs or drawings of people inside the doors and windows.
❸ Trace cookie cutters onto cork. Outline with fabric paint to make refrigerator magnets.

The Lesson Connection ...
Joshua's farewell (Joshua 23–24)
Make a model house with the words "As for me and my household, we will serve the LORD" (Joshua 24:15) written on it.

An angel visits Joseph (Matthew 1:18–25)
Make a house. Draw Joseph sleeping on a bed in 1 window and an angel in the doorway.

Supplies ...
- Roll of cork
- ½-pint milk carton
- Pencil
- Scissors
- Craft glue
- Markers

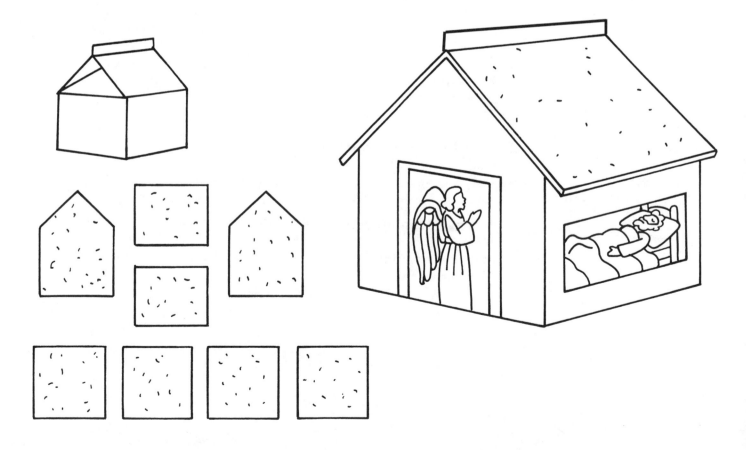

cornhusks ★★★★★★★★★★★★

Bible Doll

Supplies ...

- Dried cornhusks
- Scissors
- Thread
- Flexible wire, medium gauge
- Corn silk
- Fine-tip marker
- Glue (optional: glue gun, **adult use only**)
- Bucket of warm water

Directions ...

Buy finished cornhusks at a craft store or new ones from a grocery produce department. Dry new husks in the sun, turning every few hours. When ready to use, soak cornhusks in warm water for 15 minutes until pliable. Layer 3 husks on top of each other, narrow ends together. Fold the narrow ends over ¾". Fold over ¾" again. Fold the husks in half lengthwise. Tie a thread below the folded section to make a head. Cut 6" of wire for arms and twist over the thread. Tear ½" strips of husk and wrap them around each wire arm. Glue down the ends.

To make a robe, cut a rectangle from a husk. Cut 2 arm slits at the top. Wrap the robe around the doll and tie with thread at the neck and waist. Glue on corn-silk hair. Use fine-tipped markers to draw in a face. Add other details with dyed husks.

Options and Variations ...

❶ Cornstalks can be dyed (**by adults only**) by dissolving ½ package of fabric dye in a gallon pot of water. Add husks. Heat to a boil. Remove from heat and let sit overnight. Remove husks and dry them in the sun.

❷ Insert 2 13" strips of wire into the head and bend up ½" on the opposite ends to make legs and feet. Cut and wrap ½" strips of husks around each leg.

❸ Glue a dowel stick inside the doll to use it as a puppet.

❹ Use paper twist materials instead of cornhusks. Use yarn or artificial hair instead of corn silk.

❺ Make a simple, triangular stand from wire to hold up the doll.

The Lesson Connection ...

God blesses Ruth (Ruth)

Make a cornhusk doll to represent Ruth. Add pieces of grain to her hands. As you work, talk about how God blesses people today.

An angel visits Mary (Luke 1:26–55)

Add angel wings made from cornhusks. Tie on a raffia loop, then hang it on a Christmas tree to remind you of the many angels in the Christmas story.

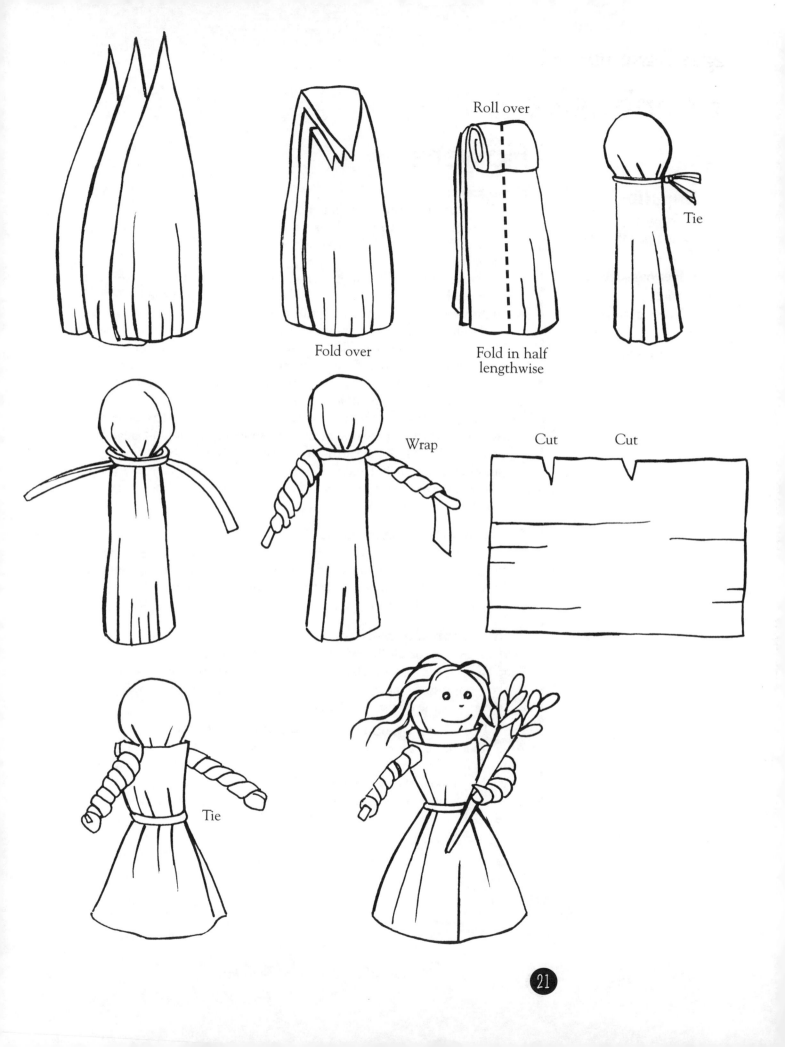

Roll over

Fold over

Fold in half
lengthwise

Tie

Wrap

Cut   Cut

Tie

cornhusks

Flowers

Supplies ...

- Dried cornhusks
- Fine-gauge floral wire
- Heavy-gauge floral wire
- Wire cutters or heavy scissors
- Floral tape

Directions ...

1. Buy finished cornhusks at craft stores or new ones in a grocery produce department. Dry new husks in the sun, turning every few hours. When ready to use, soak husks about 15 minutes in warm water until pliable.

2. To make a rose: Fold 1 husk in half, top to bottom. Hold in place, then fold and add a 2nd husk, overlapping the 1st. Roll the husks tightly from the side, pinching the base together. Add more husks to make the flower larger. Wrap fine-gauge floral wire around the base. Trim off extra wire. Trim flower base to a point. Fold 1 end of heavy-gauge wire into a hook. Insert it from the top thru the base. Gently hook the stem into the flower. Wrap green floral tape around the base of the flower and on down the stem.

3. To make a daisy: Tear husks into 1¾″ wide strips. Fold 1 strip over. Roll from the side to make the center. Wrap a piece of fine-gauge wire around the base, about 1″ from the end. Trim the wire. Fold another strip in half. Hold the ends against the center base and wrap fine-gauge wire around it. Finish by following the rose directions to add a stem (above).

Options and Variations ...

❶ Dye cornhusks (adults only): Dissolve ½ package of fabric dye in gallon pot of water. Add husks and heat to a boil. Remove from heat and let sit overnight. Remove husks and dry them in the sun.

❷ Group flowers in a bouquet.

The Lesson Connection ...

God takes care of us (Matthew 6:25–34; Luke 12:22–31)

Read the verses aloud as a class works. Help them understand that our God cares for us, giving us food, clothing, and all our earthly needs, just as he cares for the flowers and birds.

Jesus heals Peter's mother-in-law (Matthew 8:14–17)

After Jesus healed Peter's mother-in-law, she got up and began to wait on Him. Jesus freed us from sin when He died on the cross and rose from the grave. He empowers us to serve Him. Talk about people who serve us in Jesus' name—parents, teachers, pastors, leaders, janitors, bus drivers, and more. Make a flower to give as a gift to thank someone for serving you.

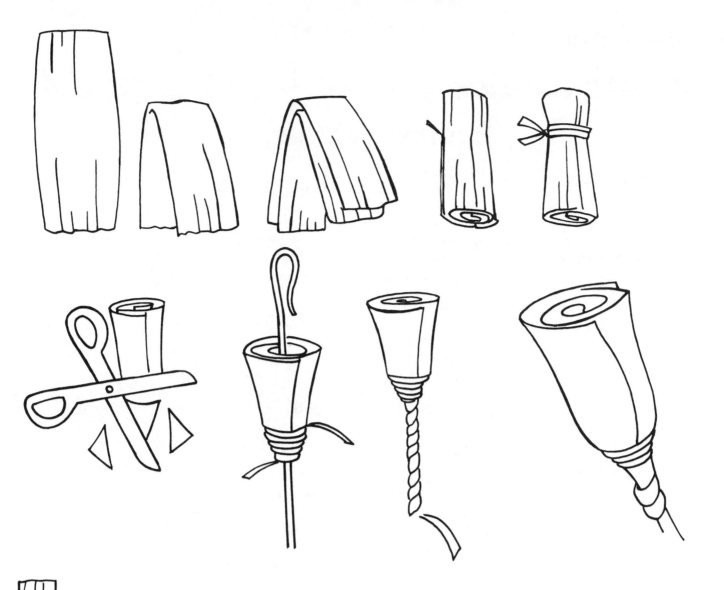

craft sticks ⭐⭐⭐⭐⭐⭐⭐⭐⭐⭐⭐

Picture Plaque

Supplies ...
- Craft sticks
- White or tacky glue
- Markers or colored glue

Directions ...
Place 10 craft sticks in a row. Glue a craft stick across the top of the row and another across the bottom. Arrange 2 sticks to make a point at the top, gluing them to the sides of the plaque and to one another at the point. Glue a craft stick on top of the last stick on each side to make a frame. With markers or glue draw a picture or write a Bible verse on the plaque. Hang by the point at the top.

Options and Variations ...
❶ Make a template on a piece of paper for young children to count and lay their sticks on.
❷ Decorate with tempera, acrylic, or fabric paint; fabric trim; glitter; or sequins. Cut and glue on cork, sandpaper, or fabric.
❸ Glue a lesson leaflet or church bulletin picture inside the plaque.
❹ Omit the point. Instead, tie on yarn, or glue a paper clip or pop-top tab on the back for hanging.
❺ Glue sticks along the bottom of the plaque for a stand-up base.

The Lesson Connection ...
Isaac and Rebekah (Genesis 24)
God made Isaac and Rebekah into a family and blessed their household. Make a picture of your house. Draw or glue on windows and a door with family members looking out of them. Or glue a family photograph in the center. Write: "God Bless the (Name) Family" on the plaque.

Jesus is born (Luke 2:1–20)
Let the plaque represent a stable. Paste a Christmas card picture in the center or draw your own manger scene.

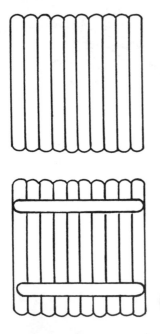
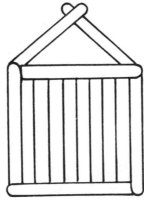

craft sticks

Puzzle

Directions ...
Place up to 10 craft sticks in a row. Tape them together with 2 rows of tape. Draw a Bible picture or passage on the sticks, then untape the sticks to take them apart and put them in an envelope. Use this puzzle to tell a story.

Options and Variations ...
❶ Let everyone make puzzles, then challenge each other to solve them.
❷ Have older students use the puzzles to teach a Bible story to younger children.

The Lesson Connection ...
David and Jonathan (1 Samuel 17:55–20:42)
Draw a heart on the sticks and write "Thank God for Friends." Put the puzzle together with a friend. As you work, talk about what makes a good friend.

Jesus teaches Mary and Martha (Luke 10:38–42)
Write a favorite verse from this story onto the sticks. Give the puzzle to a friend and tell about Jesus and His friends. Include sticks to glue onto the back of the puzzle to turn it into a plaque.

Supplies ...
• Craft sticks
• Masking tape
• Envelope
• Markers

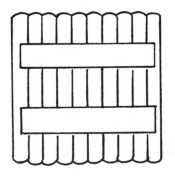

Tape

craft sticks

Glitter Cross

Supplies ...
- Notched craft sticks
- Glow-in-the-dark paint
- Craft glue
- Metallic thread
- Glitter

Directions ...
Glue 2 craft sticks to each other side by side. Glue 2 more sticks across these 2 to make a cross. Tie a metallic thread through the top hole for hanging, or use a dot of glue to attach loop of thread to back of sticks. Let dry. Paint with glow-in-the-dark paint. Lightly sprinkle glitter on the wet paint.

Options and Variations ...
❶ Glue 3 or 4 sticks in a row, instead of 2.
❷ Glue several sticks together in the center in a star pattern.
❸ Paint with tempera or acrylic paint, or dot with colored glue. Add sequins or other decorations.

The Lesson Connection ...
God keeps His promises to Abraham (Genesis 12:1–25:11)
Make a glitter cross as a reminder of the promise God made to Abraham of a descendent by whom all the world would be blessed.

The jailer at Philippi believes in Jesus (Acts 16:16–40)
Make a glow-in-the-dark cross to remind you of God's protection in dark or dangerous times.

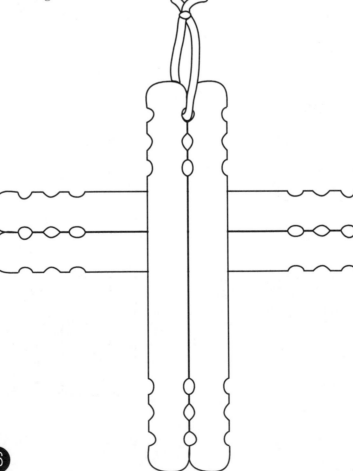

crayons

Hidden Picture

Directions ...
Pick a Bible story and think of a scene from the story to illustrate. Draw a scene on a whole sheet of paper. Fold about ⅓ of the sheet over. Draw a changed scene on the folded paper, making sure the lines match the other picture. Tell the Bible story, unfolding the hidden picture at the right time.

Options and Variations ...
❶ Make a Christmas or Easter card with a hidden picture.
❷ Cut or tear pieces of construction paper as the design.

The Lesson Connection ...
God rescues baby Moses (Exodus 2:1–10)
Draw baby Moses in a basket in the river, watched over by his sister Miriam. Draw Pharaoh's daughter on the right side of the picture. Fold the sheet over, covering Pharaoh's daughter. Finish the picture with a river scene. Start telling the story with the picture folded up. Open the flap to tell how Pharaoh's daughter found baby Moses.

Jesus stills the storm (Matthew 8:23–27)
Draw a boat in calm water in the center of the paper. Draw Jesus standing in the right side of the boat. Fold the sheet over and draw the boat in wild, wind-blown waves. Start the story with the flap folded over to show the wild waves. Open the flap to show Jesus stilling the water.

Pentecost (Acts 2:1–41)
Place the paper upright. Draw Peter and some other Christians. Draw flames of fire above their heads. Fold the top 3rd of the sheet over. Redraw the characters without the flames of fire. Open up the flap to show the flames of fire when you tell about the story.

Supplies ...
• Crayons
• Paper

crayons

Scratch Picture

Supplies ...

- Crayons
- Paper
- Newspaper
- Dark-colored tempera paint
- Paintbrush
- Stylus or paper clip
- Paper towels

Directions ...

Cover the work area with newspaper. Use crayons to heavily color stripes on a sheet of paper. Paint over the colored stripes with dark-colored tempera paint. When dry, scratch off the paint with a stylus or open paper clip to make a picture or symbol. Add words to go with the picture. Use paper towels to wipe away scraping residue.

Options and Variations ...

❶ Glue the finished picture to a piece of construction paper to frame it.
❷ Substitute India ink for dark-colored tempera.
❸ Prepare scratch pictures in advance, or buy them commercially, for younger children.

The Lesson Connection ...

God's victory at Jericho (Joshua 5:13–6:27)
Use crayons to draw bubble-shaped letters that say "Trust in the Lord." Color in the letters.

Jesus shows His glory—Transfiguration (Matthew 17:1–9)
Scratch outlines of Jesus talking to Moses and Elijah.

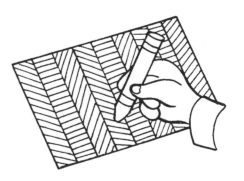

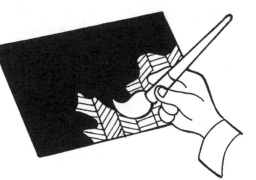

★★★★★★★★drinking straws

Memory Verse Jewelry

Directions ...
Pick colors to remind you of different parts of a Bible verse. (See The Lesson Connection for examples.) Cut straws into short lengths to form beads. Lay the beads out in color order to fit the Bible verse. If desired, repeat colors or sequence. Cut a cord 2 times longer than you want the finished piece. Tape both cord ends to make them firm enough to string beads. String the 1st 2 beads to the middle of the cord. Run the cord thru 1 of the beads again, anchoring it in place. Add beads to opposite sides, stringing the cord thru twice each time. Knot the ends of the cord together when finished.

Practice saying the Bible verse as you make your jewelry. Wear it as a reminder of the Bible verse or give it to someone as a present.

Options and Variations ...
❶ Use large beads or pasta decorated with markers as beads.
❷ Make beads from colored clay that can be baked in the oven.

The Lesson Connection ...
God made the world (Genesis 1:1–2:3)
In the beginning God (yellow) created the heavens (blue) and the earth (green).

Jesus gives us eternal life (John 3:16)
For God (yellow) so loved the world (green) that He gave His one and only Son (red), that whoever believes in Him (yellow) shall not perish (black) but have eternal life (white).

Supplies ...
- Plastic drinking straws in different colors
- Transparent tape
- Cord, elastic thread or plastic lacing
- Scissors

drinking straws ★ ★ ★ ★ ★ ★ ★ ★

Texture Picture

Supplies ...

- Drinking straws
- Poster board
- White or tacky glue
- Scissors
- Pencil
- Pop-top tab
- Tape

Directions ...

Design a Bible scene or symbol. Sketch it onto poster board. Cut straws and glue them onto the design. Glue more straws around your picture for a frame. Tape a pop-top tab to the back for a hanger.

Options and Variations ...

❶ Use different colors of straws. Add other textures by using feathers, sandpaper, sand, macaroni, etc.

❷ Have young children fit precut straws onto a pattern.

❸ Cover poster board with fabric or wallpaper before gluing on straws.

The Lesson Connection ...

God made the world (Genesis 1:1–2:3)

Make a favorite animal. (Hint: Glue several straws in a row for the body. Glue shorter lengths in rows for the neck and head.) Name the creations as the class takes turns thanking God for creating animals ("Thank You, God, for ... ").

Lydia's conversion (Acts 16:12–15)

Cut a poster-board rectangle. Sketch the name *Jesus* in block letters. Cut and glue straw pieces over the letters. Let the picture remind you that only Jesus can save us from sin.

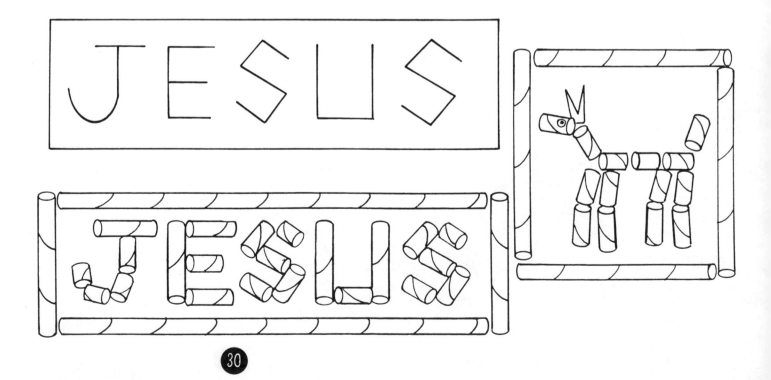

egg

Bible Figures

Directions ...
Decide what Bible character to make. Tap a hole in each end of an egg with a needle. Poke into the egg yolk to make it easier to remove. Gently blow into 1 hole. The inside of the egg will be forced out the other hole. Wash the egg; dry. Draw a face on the egg with markers. Cut and glue on paper details. Make a holder for the egg by cutting a strip of paper and gluing its ends together. Place the egg in it.

Options and Variations ...
❶ Glue on felt, cotton, yarn, or fabric scraps for hair and clothing.
❷ Glue on movable eyes.
❸ Color the blown-out egg in a mixture of food coloring, 1 cup of water, and 1 tablespoon of vinegar.
❹ Loop thread thru a button. Glue the button to the top of the egg for a hanger.

The Lesson Connection ...
God made the world (Genesis 1:1–2:3)
Make different egg animals and hang on a "creation tree."

Jesus is born (Luke 2:1–20)
Make a set of nativity figures to stand up.

Jesus rises from the dead—Easter (Luke 24:1–12; Matthew 28:1–10; 1 Corinthians 15:1–11)
A butterfly symbolizes new life and is an Easter symbol. Add paper wings to an egg to make 1. Make other eggs into a cocoon and caterpillar.

Spreading the Good News (Acts 11:19–30)
The faith of the early Christians has been handed down thru many generations to you. Make an egg of yourself and put it on a classroom "God's Family" tree.

Supplies ...
- Eggs
- Large needle
- Fine-tip markers
- Construction paper
- Glue
- Scissors

egg ★★★★★★★★★★★★★★★★

Fruits and Vegetables

Supplies ...

- Eggs
- Large needle
- Food coloring
- Vinegar
- Water
- Markers
- Green construction paper
- Glue
- Scissors

Directions ...

Tap a hole in each end of an egg with a needle. Poke into the egg yolk to make it easier to remove. Gently blow into 1 hole. The inside of the egg will be forced out the other hole. Wash the egg; dry. Dye the egg in food coloring mixed with 1 cup of water and 1 tablespoon of vinegar. Let dry. Use markers to add details. Cut and glue on paper leaves.

Options and Variations ...

❶ Write a Bible verse or prayer onto the egg.
❷ Draw a simple Bible scene onto the egg.

The Lesson Connection ...

God gives His people food and water (Exodus 16:1–17:7)
Make several favorite fruits or vegetables given by God. Place them in a basket. Weave ribbon thru a berry basket or another plastic mesh basket to make a decorative basket.

Fruit of the Spirit (Galatians 5:22–23)
Write the name of a fruit of the Spirit on each egg. Poke a pipe cleaner thru the holes. Bend up the bottom end to hold the egg and bend the top end in a loop for hanging. Hang the eggs on a "Fruit of the Spirit" tree.

★★★★★★★★★★★★ envelope

Puppet Stage

Directions ...
Seal the envelope. Cut a window as a stage in ½ of the front side. Cut a 1″ slit in the middle of the bottom edge. Draw and color a paper figure of a Bible character. Cut out the character and glue it to a craft stick. Stick the character thru the slit to tell a Bible story.

Options and Variations ...
❶ Cut a figure and background scenery from a lesson leaflet.
❷ Make a horizontal stage. Cut a slit across the whole bottom edge of the envelope. Draw faces on your fingertips, and slip them thru for a finger-puppet story.
❸ Make puppets to act out Bible verses or lesson applications.

The Lesson Connection ...
Moses and the burning bush (Exodus 3–4)
Make a puppet of Moses. Draw the burning bush on the inside of the stage window.

Jesus appears to Thomas (John 20:24–29)
Make 2 puppets—Jesus and Thomas. Cut a slit for each. Option: Draw other disciples in the window.

Supplies ...
• Envelope
• Paper
• Scissors
• Crayons, markers, or colored pencils
• Craft stick
• Glue

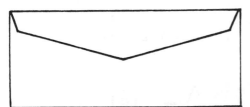

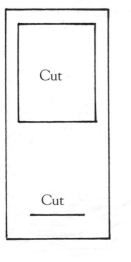

Cut

Cut

excelsior ★★★★★★★★★★★★

Bird Nest

Supplies ...

- Excelsior
- Warm water
- Paper cup
- Scissors
- Hair spray
- Ribbon
- Pom-poms (1 large, 1 smaller)
- Yellow felt
- Movable eyes
- Tacky glue

Directions ...

To make a nest: Soak excelsior in a paper cup of warm water for 30 minutes. Pour out the water. Shape the excelsior into a nest in the cup. Let dry, then remove from the cup. Trim away excess pieces with scissors. Spray with hair spray to stick pieces together. Tie ribbon into a bow and glue to the nest.

To make baby bird: Glue the larger pom-pom (bird's body) to the smaller 1 (bird's head). Cut and glue a felt beak to the smaller pom-pom. Glue on movable eyes. Glue the bird in the nest.

Options and Variations ...

❶ Buy artificial birds from a craft store.
❷ Model birds from clay or make birds from chenille wires. Or cut bird outlines from poster board and glue on feathers.
❸ Glue a ribbon or cord around the nest for hanging.

The Lesson Connection ...

God made the world (Genesis 1:1–2:3)
Use a bird-watchers guide to choose what kind of bird to make. Talk about the many different kinds of birds God made in His creation. Talk about how each person is also unique and important to God.

God takes care of us (Matthew 6:25–34; Luke 12:22–31)
As you work, talk about how baby birds depend on their parents for food. Relate this to how God gives His children the food they need. Make a bird-in-a-nest to give to a shut-in. Attach a Bible verse (e.g., Psalm 84:3–4; Psalm 17:8).

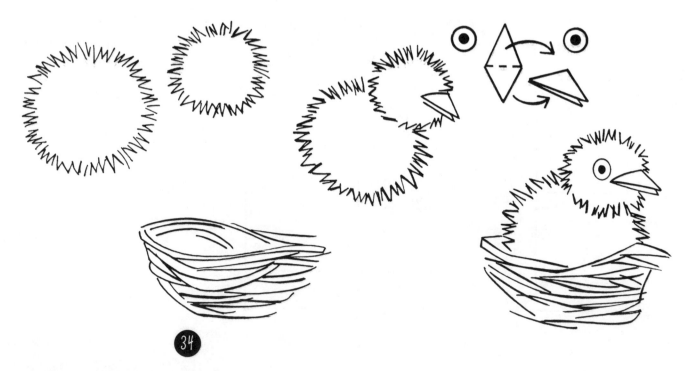

felt

Appliqué Banner

Directions ...

Draw a simple appliqué pattern on paper. Avoid hard-to-cut details. Cut out and lay on the wrong side of the felt. Outline with a pen, then cut out. Pin to a larger felt rectangle. Use embroidery floss to attach appliqué with a blanket stitch. Fold back top of the background piece; glue along edge. When dry, slip a dowel the pocket. Add yarn to each end to hang.

Blanket stitch: Thread the needle. Knot the end of the thread. Work from left to right with the lower line on the background and the upper line over the appliqué (*fig.* 1). Poke the needle thru the fabric along the lower line (*fig.* 2). Pull the thread until the knot catches. Hold the thread down with the left thumb. Now insert the needle thru the upper line, a little right of the starting point. Bring the needle out directly below, along the lower line (*fig.* 3). Draw the needle over the loop of thread (*fig.* 4). Make stitches ¼″ long and ¼″ apart. Make smaller stitches for straight edges and wider for curves.

Options and Variations ...

❶ Omit embroidery floss; attach shapes with tacky glue or fusible webbing. Use permanent markers or fabric paint to simulate stitches.

❷ Make a table runner instead of a banner. Use a round plate or lid to outline and cut out a curve along each end.

❸ Fold over the top of the banner and cut 4 parallel, equally spaced holes for the dowel stick to slip thru (*fig.* 5).

The Lesson Connection ...

God saves Noah and his family (Genesis 6:1–9:17)
Cut an ark for the center of the banner. Outline animals from animal cookies or cookie cutters, or draw your own animal shapes.

Jacob's dream (Genesis 28:10–22)
Make an embroidered angel banner. Use the pattern on page 36 to cut and glue a white angel onto dark-blue felt. Use metallic yarn to sew a blanket stitch around the angel and the outside of the felt piece. As an option, glue on felt or metallic stars. If desired, use metallic or glitter fabric paint to add details.

Supplies ...

- Felt
- Pen
- Paper
- Straight pins
- Black embroidery floss
- Embroidery needle, size 22
- Sharp fabric scissors
- Glue
- Dowel stick
- Yarn or cord

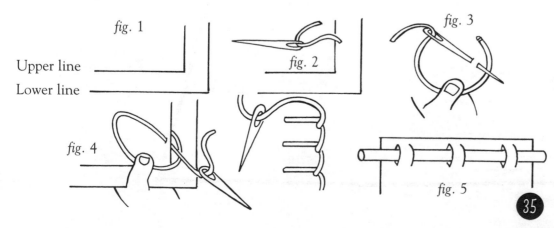

Upper line

Lower line

fig. 1

fig. 2

fig. 3

fig. 4

fig. 5

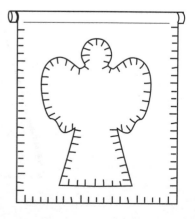

35

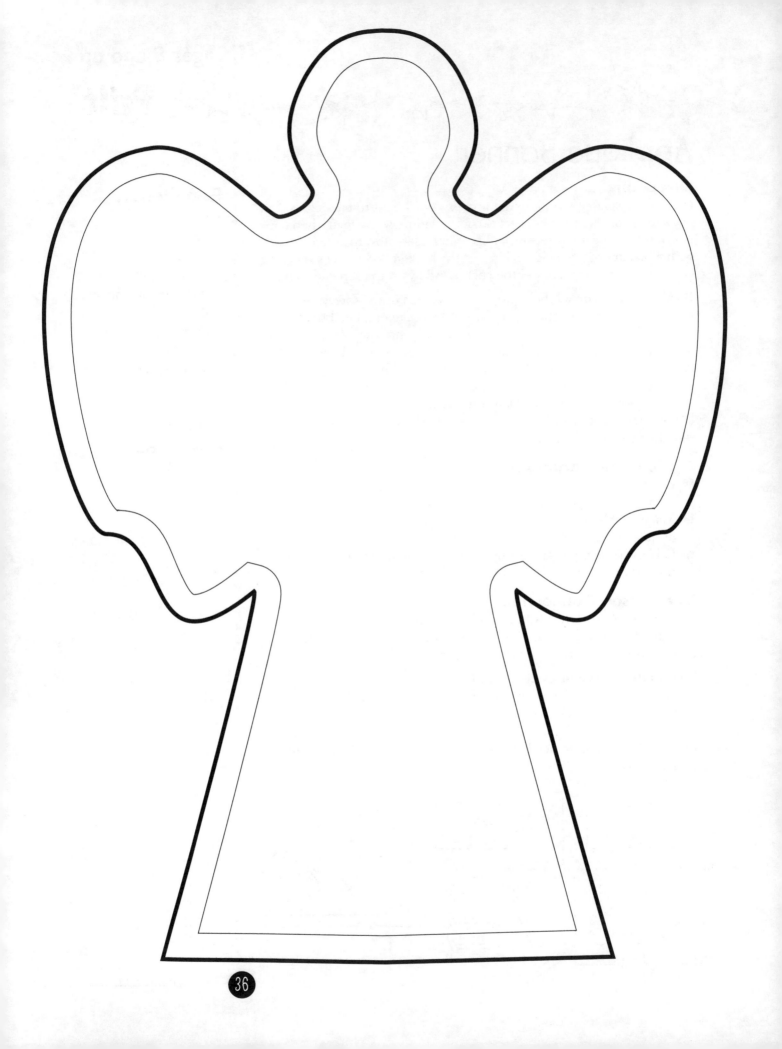

flashlight

Glow Puppet

Directions ...
Draw a face on the bag. Cut and glue fringed construction paper or yarn pieces for hair. Place the bag over a flashlight. Fasten bottom of bag around flashlight with a rubber band. Turn on the flashlight to make the face glow.

Options and Variations ...
❶ Instead of a face, draw a lighthouse or other object.
❷ Write a Bible verse on the bag. Turn on the flashlight as you read the verse.
❸ Cut a shape out of the bag. Cover the open shape with colored tissue paper or cellophane.

The Lesson Connection ...
The Ten Commandments (Exodus 19–34)
Draw a face to represent Moses. Turn on the flashlight to tell how Moses' face glowed after God gave him the Ten Commandments.

Jesus, light of the world (John 8:12)
Write the Bible verse on 1 side of the bag; draw a self-portrait on the other. Turn on the flashlight as you read the passage. Option: Write "I am God's light in the world" or "Shine for the Lord" on the bag.

Jesus is born (Luke 2:1–20)
Draw the outline of an angel on a white paper bag. Turn on the flashlight as the angel tells its message. Option: Add wings made from tissue or paper twist.

Supplies ...
• Flashlight
• Colored or brown, small paper bag
• Rubber band
• Markers or crayons
• Construction paper or yarn
• Glue
• Scissors

37

flowerpot ⭐⭐⭐⭐⭐⭐⭐⭐⭐⭐⭐⭐⭐

Angel Bell

Supplies ...
- Clay flowerpot
- Acrylic paint
- Jingle bell
- Ribbon
- Paper twist
- Metallic cord or garland
- Paintbrush
- Water in a cup
- Scissors
- Glue gun (adult use only)

Directions ...
Turn the flowerpot upside down. Paint a flesh-colored face on 1 side of the flowerpot. Paint the rest white. When dry, paint facial features. Cut a piece of ribbon and thread the jingle bell onto it. Poke the ribbon ends thru hole in the bottom (now top) of the pot. Tie a large knot over the hole. Glue down, if needed. Cut metallic cord or garland, tie in a circle, and place on top of the hair as a halo. Cut a ribbon and tie a loop, then glue it to the back as a hanger. Cut a section of paper twist. Unfold it, then twist in the middle. Glue to the back as wings.

Options and Variations ...
❶ Substitute plastic flowerpots for clay ones.
❷ Substitute Spanish moss, shredded paper, yarn, or Easter grass on top of pot as hair, instead of painting the hair.

The Lesson Connection ...
God saves Daniel's three friends (Daniel 3)
Leave off the bell and hanger. Set your angel in a spot to remind you that God's angel protects you today.

Witnesses for Jesus—Ascension (Acts 1:1–11)
Instead of drawing faces, attach religious stickers or paint on Bible passages. Attach a ribbon to the top to cover the knot. Give the bell to someone as a "witness bell" to share the Good News of Jesus.

★★★★★★★★★★★★flowerpot

Bible Character

Directions ...
Cut strips of felt to fit around the pot as shown on page 40: a flesh-colored strip for the face (a), a color strip for a headdress (b), a narrow strip of the same color for the top of the face (c), and a narrow strip to go around the rim (d). Cut a half-circle mouth (e) and a circle to fit the bottom (f). Turn the pot upside down. Glue the felt pieces on it. Glue on movable eyes and yarn for hair and/or beard. Cut and glue additional felt details, as desired.

Options and Variations ...
❶ Add paper-twist wings and a metallic chenille-wire halo to make an angel.
❷ Have an adult use a glue gun to attach a chenille-wire staff.
❸ Make a smaller face and add felt arms and hands.

The Lesson Connection ...
God saves Daniel (Daniel 6)
Make a figure with beard and hair to represent Daniel. Make a smaller flowerpot into a lion. Cut a circle of yellow felt for a face. Cut a larger ring of brown felt as a mane. Fringe the edges. Glue the face onto the mane. Add movable eyes, a triangular felt nose, and half-circle ears. Glue a yellow felt strip around the rim. Add a yarn tail with a frayed end.

Jesus is born (Luke 2:1–20)
Make figures for Mary and Joseph. Glue a chenille-wire staff to Joseph's hand. Use a smaller flowerpot to make baby Jesus in the manger. Turn the pot right-side up. Glue a strip of yellow felt around the rim. Fill the pot with excelsior. Wrap a piece of white felt around a peanut (baby Jesus in a blanket). Use a fine-tip marker to draw a face and hair on the peanut. Place baby Jesus in the excelsior.

Supplies ...
- Flowerpots
- Felt
- Yarn
- Tacky glue
- Movable eyes
- Scissors

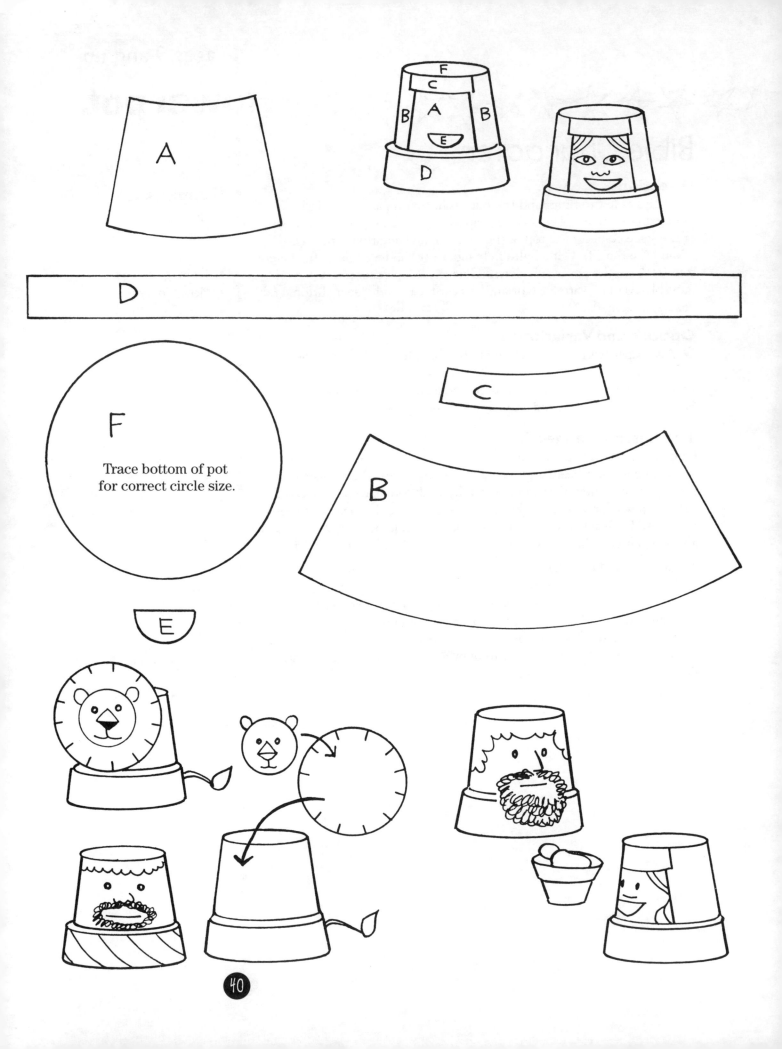

A

F

B

C

D

E

Trace bottom of pot
for correct circle size.

★★★★★★★★★★★ **frosting can**

Praise Puppet

Directions ...
Remove label from frosting can; wash. Remove lid. Draw a Bible character on the can with permanent markers. Fill with dried beans or rice; replace lid. Shake the can to have the character sing a song of praise to God.

Options and Variations ...
❶ Draw facial features on paper. Cut and glue them to the can.
❷ Cover the can with fabric or tissue paper.
❸ Write a Bible or hymn verse on the can.
❹ Have an adult seal the can with a hot glue gun.

The Lesson Connection ...
Miriam Praises God (Exodus 15:1–21)
Draw Miriam, adding a tambourine in her hands. Shake the container and sing an appropriate song, like "I Will Sing unto the Lord" from *Songs Kids Love to Sing 2* (CPH, order no. 22-2530).

Jesus enters Jerusalem—Palm Sunday (Matthew 21:1–11)
Draw pictures of the children on the can. Add palm branches and the word *Hosanna*. Shake the cans and march in a Palm Sunday parade.

Supplies ...
• Plastic frosting can
• Permanent markers
• Dried beans or rice

fun foam

Refrigerator Magnets

Supplies ...

- Fun foam
- Pencil
- Slick or glitter fabric paints
- Paint pen or permanent marker
- Scissors
- Magnetic strip
- Glue

Directions ...

Trace and cut out a fun foam shape (see patterns on page 43). Outline the shape with fabric paint. Write a phrase or Bible verse on it with a permanent marker or paint pen. Cut a magnetic strip to glue to the back. Place on refrigerator as a reminder of the lesson theme.

Options and Variations ...

❶ Cut shapes from different foam colors to glue to the larger shape.
❷ Glue on sequins or other decorative trim.
❸ Trace shapes from cookie cutters.

The Lesson Connection ...

Jesus resurrects Jairus' daughter (Mark 5:21–24, 35–43)
Jesus showed His love for Jairus' family when He raised the girl from the dead. Use this magnet to remind the students of God's love and to remind them to look for ways to show His love to others. Cut heart shapes in several sizes. Overlap smaller hearts onto a larger heart. Or outline a heart with fabric paint and write "Show God's Love" on it.

Jesus rises from the dead—Easter (Luke 24:1–12; Matthew 28:1–10; 1 Corinthians 15:1–11)
Review the life cycle of a butterfly (egg, caterpillar, cocoon, butterfly) to talk about new life. The butterfly symbolizes the resurrection. Jesus rose from the dead to give us a new life. Outline foam butterflies with fabric paint. Glue sequins on the inside of the shape.

Timothy travels with Paul and Silas (Acts 16:1–5)
Cut out a book shape. Write a favorite Bible verse on it. Use black foam for a closed Bible cover, white for an open page.

Hearts

Butterflies

Bibles

43

glass jar ★★★★★★★★★★★★★★

Candle Holder

Supplies ...

- Glass jar (baby food jars work well)
- Votive candle
- Glue
- Glitter
- Paint marker or permanent marker

Directions ...

Remove paper; clean and dry jar. Draw a pattern or picture on the outside with glue and glitter. Write a Bible verse on the jar with a paint marker. Place the votive candle inside. Use the candle for family or class devotions.

Options and Variations ...

❶ Have older children outline a pattern with leading glue (available at craft stores). Draw the design on paper 1st, then insert it in the jar for tracing. Color spaces with paint markers or glass stain.

❷ Have younger children roll a jar in glue, then glitter.

❸ Substitute salt for glitter, or add sequins. Dye salt with food coloring.

❹ Omit candle. Glue pictures from student leaflets or cards around the inside of the jar. Glue glitter or salt around them on the outside.

The Lesson Connection ...

Solomon builds the temple (1 Kings 5–8)
Outline a "stained glass" pattern on the jar. Fill spaces with colored glitter. Use your candle family worship.

Jesus, light of the world (John 8:12)
Draw a lighted candle and the Bible verse on the jar. Fill the jar with thin, metallic strips or yellow paper.

glass pane

Story Window

Directions ...

To make cleanup easy, mix a little liquid detergent with the water used to make paint with powdered tempera. Choose to paint 1 design or a series of smaller designs on the window. Outline the design with black paint. Fill in the outline with colored paint to finish the window. Use soap and water to clean the pictures off the window.

Options and Variations ...

❶ Divide the pane into a grid; paint a picture for each lesson in a unit, or week in Advent or Lent. Give each child an opportunity to paint a grid.

❷ Mark off the grids with masking tape.

The Lesson Connection ...

God made the world (Genesis 1:1–2:3)

Divide the window into 6 sections. Let small groups or individuals paint a representation of each day of creation in a section.

Jesus blesses the children (Mark 10:13–16)

Trace a circle on the window with a large pizza cardboard. Draw Jesus in the center of the circle. Have children draw themselves around Him. Write "Jesus Loves Me, This I Know" below the picture. Use the picture to witness to the love of Jesus present in your classroom.

Supplies ...

- Glass pane
- Powdered tempera paint
- Dishwashing detergent
- Rag for cleanup

JESUS LOVES ME, THIS I KNOW

glue ★ ★ ★ ★ ★ ★ ★ ★ ★ ★ ★ ★ ★ ★ ★ ★ ★ ★

Promise Reminder

Supplies ...
- White glue
- Plastic lid
- Sequins or other decorations
- Needle and thread

Directions ...
Pour white glue into a plastic lid. Make a pattern in the glue with sequins or other decorations. Let dry about 3 days. Remove from the lid. Poke a threaded needle thru the top. Tie the thread to make a hanger. Use as an ornament, a wall hanging, or a suncatcher.

Options and Variations ...
❶ Use beads, small rocks, macaroni, spices, nuts, dried flowers, or colored cellophane.
❷ Make edgeless reminders by pouring glue on waxed paper.
❸ Cover a cardboard piece with waxed paper. Pin metallic cord in a shape. Fill the shape with glue.
❹ Use colored glue. Make your own by adding food coloring to white glue.

The Lesson Connection ...
God rescues Adam and Eve (Genesis 3)
Adam and Eve's fall into sin was followed by the promise of a Savior. As a reminder of God's promise, make a cross in the center. Add different materials on the rim and space between.

Pentecost (Acts 2:1–41)
Make a flame from red, transparent, plastic beads. Fill the rest of the lid with a different color. Hang it as a visual reminder of the power of God's Spirit in the Christian's life.

golf tee

Mini Puppet

Directions ...
Glue a wooden bead to top of a tee. Draw facial features with markers on the bead. Cut and glue on craft hair. Cut and glue on clothing from fabric or paper scraps. Stand up your figures in clay or Styrofoam.

Options and Variations ...
❶ Twist a piece of ribbon together in the center. Glue to the back of the tee to make an angel. Add a metallic halo.
❷ Draw clothing with markers.

The Lesson Connection ...
God protects Joseph (Genesis 37; 39–41)
Change the head from 1 tee to another to tell the story of Joseph. On the 1st tee, draw Joseph's coat of many colors with permanent markers. Draw Egyptian-style clothes on a 2nd tee.

An angel visits Zechariah (Luke 1:5–25)
Make an angel, using a metallic ribbon bow and metallic cord halo. Add curly hair.

Supplies ...
• Golf tee
• Wooden bead
• Craft glue
• Fine-tipped permanent markers
• Craft hair
• Fabric or paper scraps
• Scissors

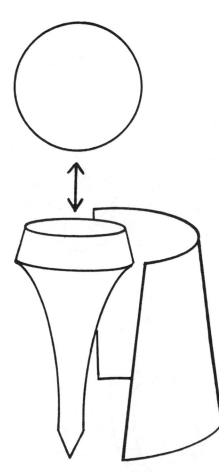

jar lid ★★★★★★★★★★★★★★★★★★★

Prayer Reminder

Supplies ...
- Jar lid
- Bible picture
- Glue
- Poster board
- Scissors

Directions ...
Cut a picture to fit inside the lid. Glue it in place. Cut a triangle from poster board. Fold it as shown and glue the folded point to the back of the jar lid.

Options and Variations ...
❶ Glue several lids down a strip of ribbon to make a banner.
❷ Glue decorative trim around the rim of the lid.

The Lesson Connection ...
Hezekiah prays to God (2 Kings 20:1–11)
Write "Pray to the Lord" on a piece of paper to glue inside the lid. Add dried flowers. (To dry flowers, hang them upside down for 1 or 2 weeks in a cool, dry place.) Tie a raffia bow around the lid, or glue it to the bottom or top of the lid.

Jesus came for everyone (Acts 10:1–11:18)
Glue a picture of Jesus onto a piece of paper that fits into the lid. Around it write, "Jesus Came for (Your Name)."

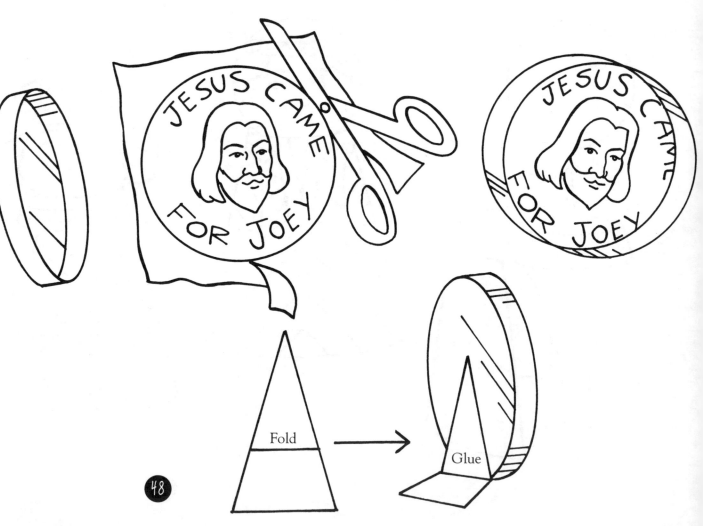

leaves

Bible Verse Picture

Directions ...

Lay out the leaves (and flowers) in a design on a piece of paper. Use a pencil to lightly outline the design. Paint the back of a leaf in the design and place it carefully on the paper. Smooth it down with a paper towel. Carefully remove the leaf. Repeat with the same or different leaves until the pattern is filled in. Use a marker to write a Bible phrase or verse on the paper.

Options and Variations ...

❶ Use this method to make a Christian greeting card.
❷ Use metallic or glitter fabric paint.
❸ Add glitter or salt to wet prints for a different look.

The Lesson Connection ...

God cares for Jacob (Genesis 28:10–33:20)
Respond to God's care for us by making a card to show care for a shut-in person. Make a leaf and flower print on the front. Write "God Cares for You" on the inside.

The crown of life (Revelation 2:10)
Print a circle of leaves with metallic fabric paint to make a crown. Write the Bible verse on the inside.

Supplies ...

- Fresh leaves
- Fresh flowers (optional)
- Paper
- Pencil
- Tempera or poster paint
- Paintbrush
- Paper towel
- Markers

GOD CARES FOR YOU!

matchbox ★ ★ ★ ★ ★ ★ ★ ★ ★ ★

Bible Memory Box

Supplies ...

- Empty matchbox
- Black construction paper
- White paper
- Pen or pencil
- Glue
- Pasta alphabet letters
- Scissors

Directions ...

Glue white paper to 1 large side of a matchbox. Cut and glue black construction paper pieces to the other sides. Glue alphabet letters to spell "Holy Bible" to the white paper. Cut paper to fit in the inside the box. Write Bible verses on the paper to place inside the box.

Options and Variations ...

❶ Glue letters to spell "Good News" or "A Love Letter" to the box.

❷ Cover the boxes with a paper color that matches classroom or personal Bibles.

❸ Store memory verses from a lesson or unit of study. Make copies of verses for younger children.

❹ Use the verses for classroom opening or family devotions.

❺ Paraphrase Bible verses to put inside the Bible.

❻ Make gift Bibles with comforting passages to give to shut-ins or others with special concerns.

❼ Make a "Witness Bible" with passages that tell about Jesus. Share it with someone who does not know Jesus.

❽ Write a passage for each day of the week. Use them for personal devotions.

The Lesson Connection ...

Solomon's prayer (1 Kings 3:1–15; 4:29–34)

God granted Solomon great wisdom. Write verses from his wisdom sayings in the book of Proverbs.

Jesus teaches Mary and Martha (Luke 10:38–42)

Mary sat at Jesus' feet to learn. We learn from Jesus thru the Bible. Use the matchbox Bible to keep passages that tell about Jesus and His love for the world.

matchbox

Pop-Up Puppet

Directions ...
Glue paper to cover the matchbox. Draw a picture on the top of the matchbox cover. Draw a picture inside the box. Use the pop-up puppet to tell the Bible story.

Options and Variations ...
❶ Draw a speech balloon in the box. Open the box to show what the person on the cover is saying.
❷ Draw a picture on the cover to go with a Bible passage on the box.
❸ Draw angels inside the box. Open the box to make the angels appear.

The Lesson Connection ...
God saves Noah and his family (Genesis 6:1–9:17)
Glue blue paper on the cover, then draw an ark on top. Draw Noah on deck. Draw rows of animals inside the box. As you tell the story, push the animals into the ark, then push them out again.

God rescues baby Moses (Exodus 2:1–10)
Glue yellow paper on the top of the cover and blue paper on all sides. Draw reeds on the sides and basket weave on top. Draw baby Moses inside the box. Put the pieces together to float Moses on the river. Open the box to tell how he was found.

Pentecost (Acts 2:1–41)
Turn the matchbox vertically. Draw Peter's face on the cover top. Draw a flame inside. Push up the flame as you tell the story.

Supplies ...
- Empty matchbox
- Paper
- Scissors
- Glue
- Fine-tipped markers

milk carton ⭐⭐⭐⭐⭐⭐⭐⭐⭐⭐⭐

Boat Bowl

Supplies ...

- Milk carton
- Scissors
- Brown grocery sack
- Nontoxic glue
- Markers
- Snack crackers or cookies

Directions ...

Wash carton thoroughly. Cut in half from top to bottom (*fig. 1*). Cut and glue paper strips from a grocery sack to the carton to represent boards. Add details (e.g., grain, knotholes) with markers. Fill with crackers or cookies to share a snack with the class. As you eat, talk about how God gives you food and all good gifts (James 1:17).

Options and Variations ...

❶ Make a basket. Cut the carton in half across the middle (*fig. 2*). Add a cardboard or yarn handle.
❷ Cover the carton with patterned adhesive-backed paper.
❸ Line the bowl with plastic wrap or insert a sandwich bag to hold the snacks.
❹ Write a table prayer or Bible verse on the boat.

The Lesson Connection ...

God saves Noah and his family (Genesis 6:1–9:17)
Cut a carton in half from top to bottom (*fig. 1*). Cut 2 slits in the middle of a cut side to make a gangplank that will open and close. Cut another carton in half across the middle (*fig. 2*). Set the top of this carton inside the 1st carton. Decorate both parts to look like wood. Give animal crackers to the children (have them wash their hands well), and let them march the animals in and out of the ark before eating them.

The great catch of fish (John 21:1–14)
Add fish crackers to your boat.

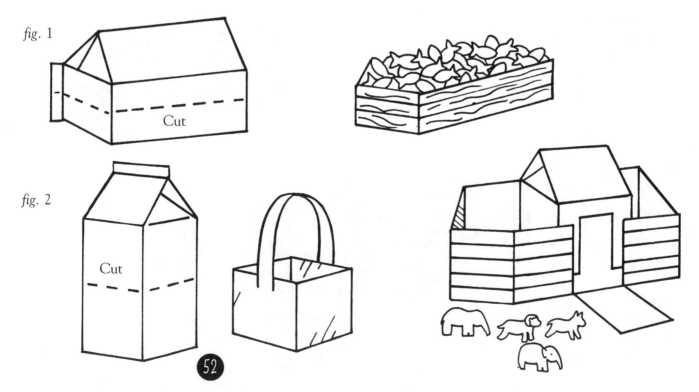

fig. 1

fig. 2

★★★★★★☆ modeling compound

Bead Necklace

Directions ...

Roll different colors of modeling compound into "snakes." Twist 2 or more "snakes" together, then wrap around a knitting needle. Push "snakes" together on the needle and roll until they are an even size. Use a knife to cut the compound into beads, then remove from the needle. Cut a shape bead (e.g., heart, cross) from flattened dough. Poke a hole at the top. Bake beads on cookie sheet according to package directions. String beads on a cord with the ends reinforced by tape. Wear the necklace or give it to someone else.

Options and Variations ...

❶ String beads on a leather cord, a shoelace, or a ribbon.

❷ Use a rolling pin to roll out thin layers of color. Wrap layers on top of each other on the knitting needle. Roll the layers together.

❸ Use a miniature cookie cutter to cut a shape bead.

❹ Roll 2 colors into "snakes," then twist together. Combine 2 lengths to form a cross. Flatten and stamp it with a pattern.

The Lesson Connection ...

God rescues Adam and Eve (Genesis 3)
Make a cross necklace as a reminder that God rescued all people from sin thru Jesus' death and resurrection. Roll a larger bead for the center. Flatten slightly and imprint a cross on it.

Jesus teaches about love (Luke 6:27–38)
Cut a heart-shaped bead. Imprint a cross in it. Use it as a center medallion when stringing your necklace. Let it remind you to live a life of Christian love.

Supplies ...

- Modeling compound
- Knitting needle
- Knife
- Cookie sheet
- Oven
- Cord
- Transparent tape

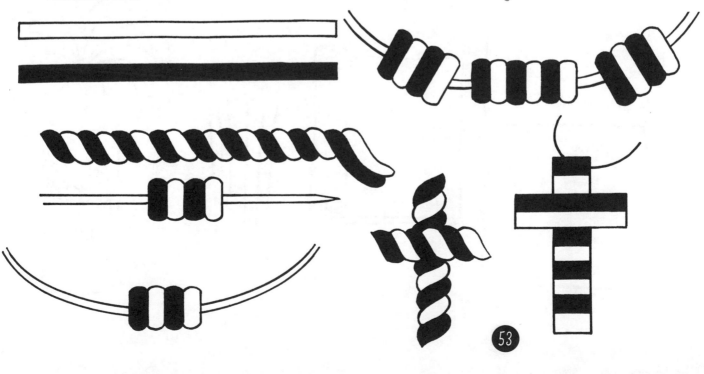

newspaper ★★★★★★★★★★★

Growing Tree

Supplies ...
- Newspaper
- Large cardboard tube (paper-towel size or larger)
- Brown paper
- Glue
- Markers
- Scissors

Directions ...
Cut and glue brown paper to cover the tube. Write a phrase on the tube with a marker. Fold a full newspaper sheet in half, then roll it up. Make long cuts around the roll. Apply glue to the outside of the uncut end, and insert the whole roll in the tube. The natural unrolling of the roll should stick the paper to the tube. Let dry. When ready to use, pull out the fringed newspaper to show a growing tree.

Options and Variations ...
❶ Substitute green construction paper, tissue, or wrapping paper for newspaper.
❷ Cover the tube with wood-grained adhesive paper.
❸ Make a forest of trees by setting them on the upright pegs of a ring toss game or boot tree.

The Lesson Connection ...
The tree growing by the water (Psalm 1)
Write words from Psalm 1:1–3 around the tube. Pull out the branches as you read the words. Stand up the tree as a reminder to stay connected to God and His Word.

The mustard seed (Mark 4:30–32)
Write "God's Kingdom Grows" on the tube. Use it as a storytelling aid.

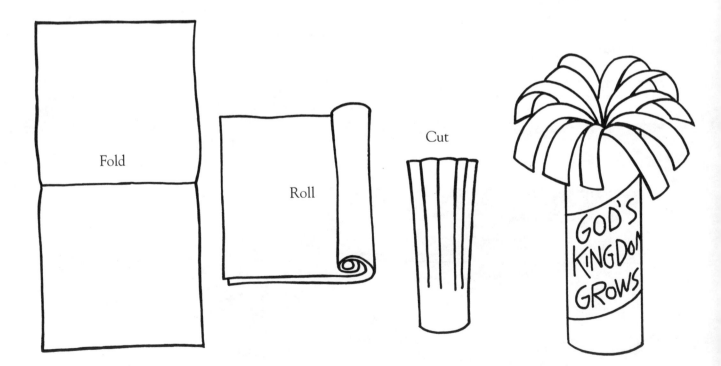

Fold

Roll

Cut

GOD'S KINGDOM GROWS

★ ★ ★ ★ ★ ★ ★ ★ ★ ★ ★ ★ **oatmeal box**

Arm Puppet

Directions ...
Remove lid from box. Turn box upside down. Cover box with construction paper. Cut a skin-colored oval for a face or use the patterns on page 56. Draw facial features. Cut and glue on paper hair and/or a beard. Glue the face to the box. Draw, cut, and glue arms and hands to the sides. Stick your hand inside the box to use as a puppet.

Options and Variations ...
❶ Use these materials for covering the box: wrapping paper, fabric, wallpaper, felt, adhesive-backed paper.
❷ Make yarn or cotton-ball hair.
❸ Glue a stick to the inside wall to use as a stick puppet.
❹ Attach self-adhesive dots for eyes and half a dot as a mouth.

The Lesson Connection ...
God's victory at Jericho (Joshua 5:13–6:27)
Make a puppet to represent Joshua, telling how God helped him at Jericho. Add other puppets as Levites and soldiers. Let your students present this puppet story to another group or as a children's sermon in worship.

Jesus is born (Luke 2:1–20)
Make puppets for Mary and Joseph. Cover a smaller, round container, such as deodorant bottle, to make baby Jesus. Cut a small box in half and glue back-to-back to make a manger. Move the puppets on a tabletop while you tell the story. Add other figures and leave them assembled as a classroom manger set.

Supplies ...
- Round oatmeal box
- Construction paper
- Pencil
- Scissors
- Glue
- Markers or crayons

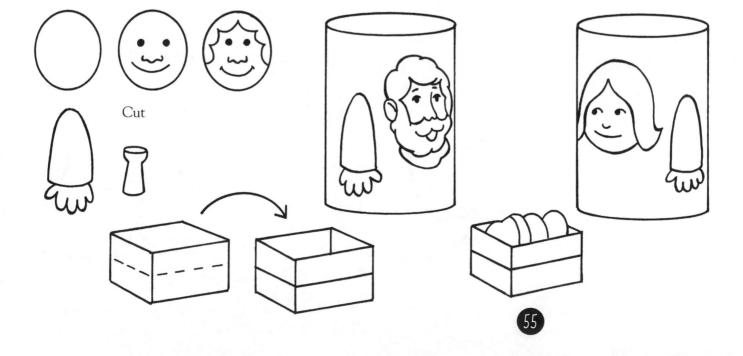

Cut

orange

Star Medallion

Directions ...
Have an adult cut orange slices about ¼" thick. Place them on a drying rack or cookie sheet. Bake 2 hours at 200°F. After 2 hours the oranges will be leathery, though still soft and a little sticky. Air dry in a warm, dry place for a week. Punch a hole in the rind with a needle. Tie a ribbon thru it for hanging. If time is short, prepare the slices ahead of time. Find the star shape in the center of the slice with the children.

Options and Variations ...
❶ Use fruit that is getting old and dry.
❷ Substitute grapefruits.
❸ Attach a dried slice to a stick to make a flower.
❹ Brush food coloring on before baking.
❺ Include the star in an arrangement of dried weeds and pine cones.

The Lesson Connection ...
God calls Isaiah (Isaiah 6:1–8)
Isaiah prophesied about the coming of the Savior. Make an orange medallion to remember that Jesus was to be the "Light for the Gentiles" (Isaiah 42:6–7). See and smell the medallion to remember that Jesus came to be light for all people.

Mary anoints Jesus (Mark 14:3–9; John 12:1–8)
Make an orange flower to remember to grow in the "sweet-smelling" gift of love for Jesus. Stick a dowel into the side of a dried orange slice. Place the other end of the stick into a piece of foam in the bottom of a flower-pot. Write an appropriate Bible passage on the side of the flowerpot.

Supplies ...
- Orange
- Knife
- Ribbon
- Cookie sheet or drying rack
- Large needle
- Ribbon

paint stick

Stick Puppet

Supplies ...
- Paint stick
- Craft sticks
- Markers
- Felt or fabric scraps
- Glue

Directions ...
Draw a face and body on the top part of the paint stick. Glue 2 craft sticks to the paint stick to represent arms. Cover the body and arms with fabric or felt. Hold the bottom of the paint stick to move the puppet.

Options and Variations ...
❶ Glue a figure cut from poster board or a leaflet onto the paint stick.
❷ Add cotton-ball hair and felt hands.

The Lesson Connection ...
David and Saul (1 Samuel 18–26)
Make David and King Saul puppets. Have children write dialog to tell their story.

Paul becomes a Christian (Acts 9:1–20)
Draw an angry Saul on 1 side of the paint stick and a happy Paul on the other. Flip the stick around to tell the story of Paul's conversion.

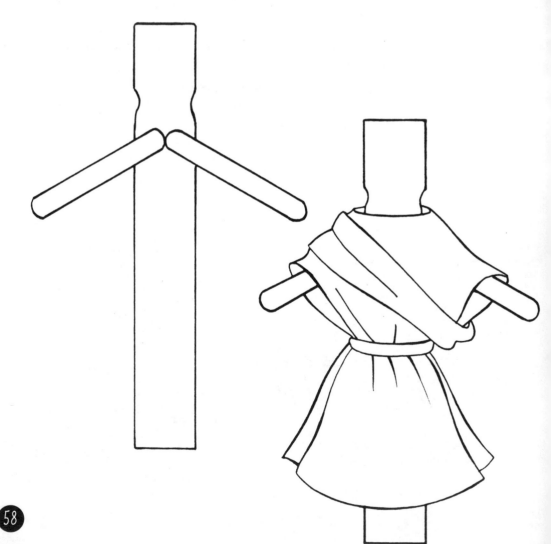

paper

Lantern

Directions ...

Accordion-fold a sheet of paper. Make small pleats to allow smaller, more frequent shapes on the folds. Make larger pleats to make larger shapes. Sketch symmetrical shapes on the fold lines, then cut them out. Unfold the paper. Write a Bible verse or phrase on the top or bottom edge. Glue the paper ends to make a circle. Punch 2 holes on the top and tie a piece of yarn thru them for hanging.

Options and Variations ...

❶ Shine a flashlight thru the lantern.

❷ Glue 2 different paper colors together. Use metallic wrapping paper for 1 of them.

❸ Cover a tin can with colored paper, then glue the lantern to it to make a pencil holder.

❹ Fold the paper lengthwise.

The Lesson Connection ...

God calls Cain to repent (Genesis 4:1–16)

Cut cross shapes to remember that all people sin and need God's forgiveness in Christ.

Paul shows love to Onesimus and Philemon (Philemon)

Cut hearts to remember that God's love shines in a Christian's life.

Supplies ...

- Paper
- Pencil
- Scissors
- Glue
- Paper punch
- Yarn
- Markers

Fold

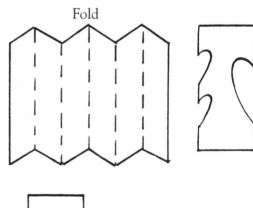

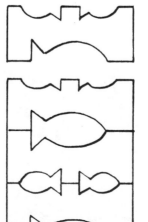

GLOW WITH GOD'S LOVE

paper ☆✫☆✫☆✫☆✫☆✫☆✫☆✫☆✫☆

Pop-Up Card

Supplies ...
- 2 sheets of paper
- Scissors
- Pencil
- Glue
- Colored markers, pencils, or crayons

Directions ...
Fold paper in half (*fig.* 1). Cut a slit in from the fold (*fig.* 2). Fold a triangle forward and score the fold line (*fig.* 3). Fold the triangle in the opposite direction and score the fold again (*fig.* 4). Open the card (*fig.* 5). Carefully push the triangle thru to the inside of the card, making it pop up on the center fold. Fold the rest of the card together. The outside will look like *figure* 4. Sketch a design using the triangle, which will pop up when the card opens. Glue another piece of paper to the outside to cover the pop-up mechanism (*fig.* 6).

The Lesson Connection ...
Jesus is born (Luke 2:1–20)
Draw an angel, stable, bell, or manger from the triangle shape with markers, crayons, or colored pencils. Add a Christmas greeting or Bible verse. As you work, talk about what it might have been like to have been a shepherd on the 1st Christmas. The shepherds shared the Good News of Jesus' birth, and so can you. Give your card to someone else.

Jesus rises from the dead—Easter (Luke 24:1–12; Matthew 28:1–10; 1 Corinthians 15:1–11)
Use an angel pop-up to announce the news of Jesus' resurrection.

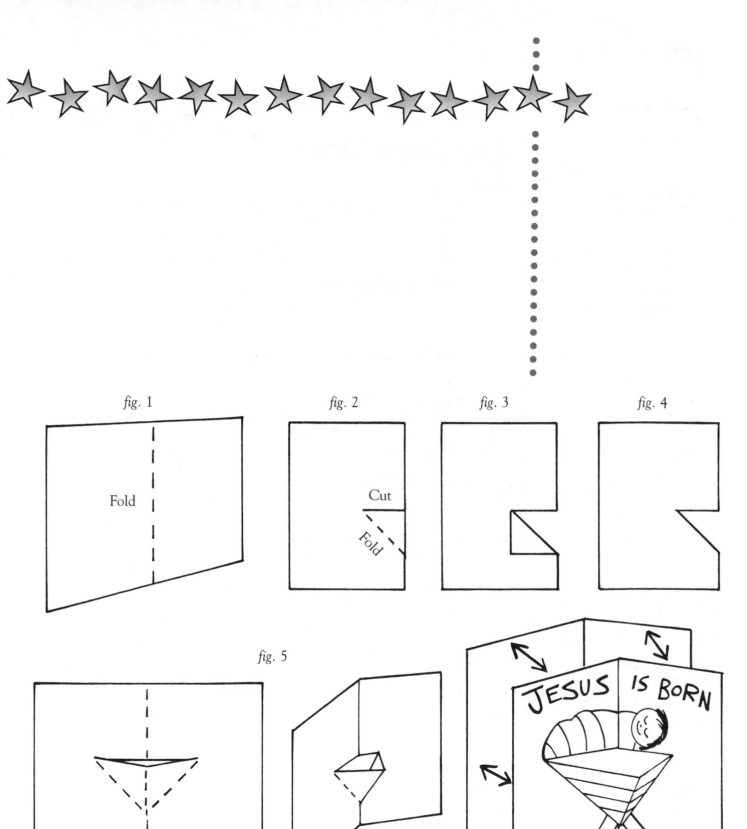

fig. 1

Fold

fig. 2

Cut

Fold

fig. 3

fig. 4

fig. 5

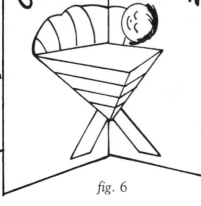

JESUS IS BORN

fig. 6

paper

3-D Sculptures

Supplies ...
- Colored paper (heavier weight works best)
- Pencil
- Scissors
- Markers, pencils, or crayons

Directions ...
Fold paper in half. Trace around the chosen pattern or draw your own design, making sure it has a base. Cut and fold the lines as shown on the pattern. Alternate creases, folding rows back and forth. Decorate with markers, colored pencils, crayons, or scraps of colored paper.

Options and Variations ...
❶ For younger children: Trace the pattern for them to cut out.
❷ Glue different colors of paper together with rubber cement before cutting.
❸ Let older children experiment with designs by cutting different lines and angles.

The Lesson Connection ...
God saves Noah and his family (Genesis 6:1–9:17)
Make an ark and decorate it. Or, make a dove to resemble the dove that found dry land.

Jesus dies for us (Mark 15)
Make a cross from purple (to show Jesus as king), black (to represent death), or brown (wood-colored) paper.

Jesus rises from the dead—Easter (Mark 16:1–8)
Make a cross from brightly colored paper. Glue cutouts of grass and flowers to the base.

Jesus and Zacchaeus (Luke 19:1–10)
Cut out a heart with a cross to remember Jesus' love for sinners.

Jesus raises Lazarus (John 11:1–45)
Write "I am the resurrection and the life" on the base of the cross. Wad or twist pieces of colored tissue and glue them on.

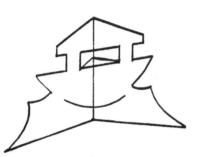

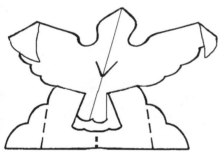

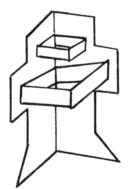

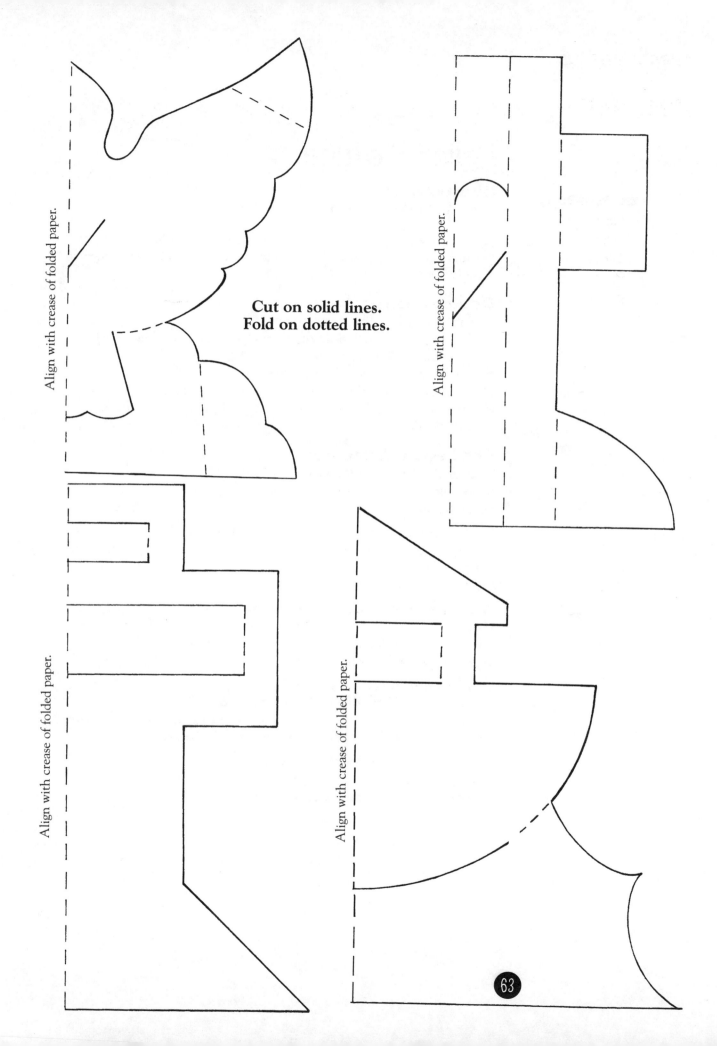

Align with crease of folded paper.

Cut on solid lines.
Fold on dotted lines.

Align with crease of folded paper.

Align with crease of folded paper.

Align with crease of folded paper.

63

paper ☆☆☆☆☆☆☆☆☆☆☆

Relief Picture

Supplies ...
- Paper
- Scissors
- Glue
- Pencil and paper

Directions ...
Experiment making some of these shapes with paper strips.

Sketch a design on paper, using some of these shapes. Cut paper strips and make the shapes. Glue them together and to the paper to make your design.

Options and Variations ...
❶ Substitute ribbon for paper strips.
❷ Attach paper coils to drinking straws, craft sticks, or dowel sticks to make flowers. Arrange in a vase.
❸ Use heavy paper to make stand-up shapes.
❹ Hang shapes with thread to make decorations for a tree.
❺ Make a mobile by hanging several shapes from a hanger or dowel stick.

The Lesson Connection ...
God made the world (Genesis 1:1–2:3)
Make a creation mobile. Attach the shapes representing things God has made to a hanger.

Jesus walks on water (Matthew 14:22–33)
Use blue strips to represent water, a brown strip for the boat, circles for the disciples' heads, and a long triangle with a circle on top for Jesus. Glue them to blue paper.

Our good shepherd cares for us (John 10:1–18)
Glue circles together to make a sheep. Add an oval for a head, a triangle for an ear, and rectangles for legs. Hang from a green triangle with the words "Jesus' Little Lamb" written on it.

Jesus is born (Luke 2:1–20) or
Jesus rises from the dead—Easter (John 20:1–18)
Fill a paper circle with a simple shape representing the season (e.g., angel, stable, star, butterfly, flower). Tie on a thread for hanging.

The first Christians (Acts 2:42–47)
Outline a fish. Shape paper strips to form the word *Jesus*. Use the fish outline to illustrate other Bible stories involving fish.

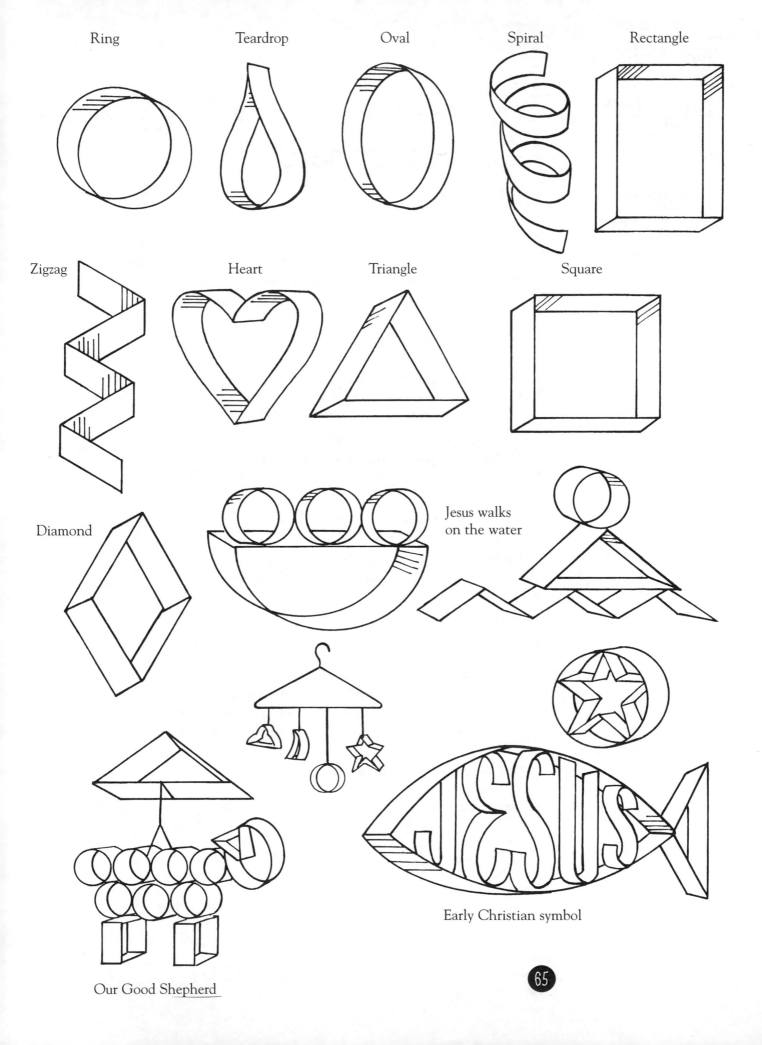

Ring

Teardrop

Oval

Spiral

Rectangle

Zigzag

Heart

Triangle

Square

Diamond

Jesus walks
on the water

Our Good Shepherd

Early Christian symbol

65

paper ☆ ✦ ☆ ✦ ☆ ✦ ☆ ✦ ☆ ✦ ☆ ✦ ☆

Supplies ...
- Paper square
- Markers, crayons, or colored pencils
- Glue (optional)

Origami Puppets

Directions ...

Fold a paper square in half across the diagonal to make a triangle. Place the triangle in front of you, folded side up. Fold the top corners up or down. The angle of the fold determines the puppet type. If needed, glue down the folds. Draw in facial features. Use large paper squares to make hand puppets, small squares for finger puppets. Tell a Bible story with the puppet. Have the children use the puppet to tell the story to their friends and family.

Options and Variations ...

❶ For younger children, draw dotted fold lines.

❷ Add fabric and/or yarn details to the puppets. Glue on movable eyes.

❸ Glue the head to a craft stick to make a stick puppet or to a cardboard tube or small box to make a stand-up puppet.

The Lesson Connection ...

God protects Joseph (Genesis 37; 39–41)
Fold down the corners to make Egyptian-style hair. Fold up the bottom point to make a chin. Add facial features.

Balaam blesses Israel (Numbers 22–24)
Fold up the corners to make Balaam's donkey's ears. Draw facial features.

Kings worship Jesus (Matthew 2:1–12)
Fold the corners in to make a turban. Draw facial features, including a beard.

Jesus resurrects Jairus' daughter (Mark 5:21–24, 35–43)
Fold down the corners to make hair. Fold the point back to make a chin. Draw facial features.

Jesus stills the storm (Matthew 8:23–27)
Turn the triangle with the fold open to the top. Fold the corners up to the top point. Turn the square over. Fold back the bottom point. Draw in the boat outline and mast. Draw Jesus and His disciples inside the boat. Move the boat as you tell the story.

Jesus rises from the dead—Easter (Luke 24:1–12; Matthew 28:1–10; 1 Corinthians 15:1–11)
Turn the triangle so the fold is to the bottom. Fold up the 2 bottom corners to make flower petals. Write "My Savior Lives" on the flower. Glue a craft stick to back. Add a green paper stem and leaves.

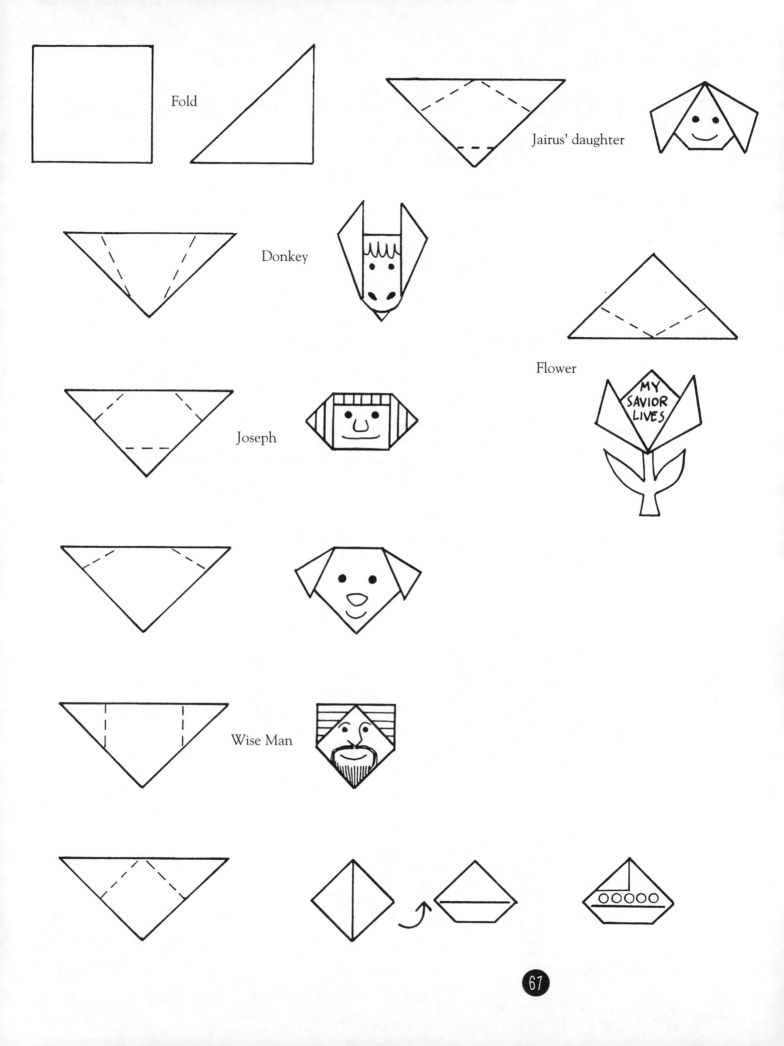

Fold

Jairus' daughter

Donkey

Flower

MY
SAVIOR
LIVES

Joseph

Wise Man

paper bag ⭐⭐⭐⭐⭐⭐⭐⭐⭐⭐⭐⭐⭐

Puppet

Supplies ...

- Paper bag
- Paper
- Markers or crayons
- Glue
- Scissors

Directions ...

Choose a Bible character to make as a puppet. Trace and/or enlarge, color, and cut out a face and body pattern from page 69 or design your own. Cut the face in half at the mouth. Glue the top part of the face to the bottom of the flat bag. Glue the body about ½″ under the fold. Glue the bottom half of the face onto the body, matching up the edges. Use your puppet to tell the story of the Bible figure it represents.

Options and Variations ...

❶ Glue on details from construction paper, wrapping paper, wallpaper, and/or fabric. Add hair and/or a beard with cotton or yarn.

❷ Use a lunch-sized bag for a smaller puppet, and a full-sized grocery bag for body-sized puppets.

The Lesson Connection ...

God keeps His people safe (Esther)

Draw a woman puppet with a crown to represent Queen Esther. Cover the bag with fabric and glue on yarn hair. Glue aluminum foil or glitter over the crown. As you work, talk about how God uses people to help others.

Jesus teaches about greatness (Matthew 18:1–9)

Make a puppet to represent Jesus. Use it to tell His story.

Girl or Boy

Jesus

Woman

69

paper bag ☆☆☆☆☆☆☆☆☆☆☆☆

Fish

Supplies ...

- Paper bag
- Markers or crayons
- Newspaper
- String
- Paper scraps
- White glue
- Scissors
- Pencil
- Paper punch

Directions ...

Draw a fish on a paper bag, adding eyes, fins, mouth, and scales with markers, crayons, and/or paper scraps. Write a Bible verse on the fish from the related Bible story. Stuff the fish with wadded newspaper. Tie a piece of string near the open end of the bag to make a tail. Punch a hole at the top and tie string thru it for hanging. As you work, talk about the Bible story.

Options and Variations ...

❶ Draw details with light-colored crayons, then cover with a watercolor wash for a crayon resist.
❷ Use metallic paper or large sequins for scales.
❸ Use circular stickers for eyes; cut them in half for scales.
❹ Decorate stuffed bags to make other kinds of animals.
❺ Stick 1 end of a dowel in plastic-based clay and the other in a slit cut in the fish to stand it up.
❻ Mount a fish made from a small bag on a Styrofoam tray or paper plate. Write the Bible phrase or passage around it.

The Lesson Connection ...

Jonah preaches in Ninevah (Jonah)
Draw an outline of Jonah praying on 1 side of the fish. Write, "God Heard Jonah Pray" on a piece of paper attached to the fish's mouth.

The great catch of fish (John 21:1–14)
Write "Trust in the Lord" on the fish to remember to trust God for all earthly needs.

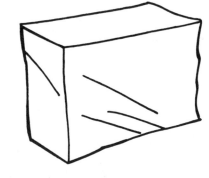

paper bag

Wig and Beard

Directions ...
Pick a Bible character to represent. Cut a face hole in the bag. (Cut out just the upper face to make a bearded man.) Cut fringes in the hair and beard. Rub the end of the scissors along the strips to curl the hair. Paint the hair and beard, if desired. Wear them to pretend to be a character telling a Bible story.

Options and Variations ...
❶ Add details with a marker, crayon, or construction paper.
❷ Make an animal head. To make a sheep, cut a face hole, glue on white ears, and glue cotton balls over the bag.
❸ Glue on paper or fabric for clothes.

The Lesson Connection ...
Samson the judge (Judges 13–15)
Cut the wig into long, curling strips. Make a 2nd bag with short hair to depict Samson without hair, or have another person cut off Samson's hair as the story is told.

Jesus accepts a Samaritan woman (John 4:1–42)
Make a wig for the Samaritan woman to wear as she tells the story of Jesus talking to her at the town well.

Supplies ...
- Paper bag (grocery size)
- Scissors
- Tempera paint
- Paintbrush

paper cup

Puppet with a Crown

Supplies ...
- 2 Styrofoam cups
- Glue
- Scissors
- Permanent markers
- Construction paper

Directions ...
Cut a zigzag crown from the base of 1 cup. Turn the 2nd cup upside down. Draw facial features on it with markers. Glue the crown onto it. Cut and glue on paper hair, clothing, and arms, as desired.

Options and Variations ...
❶ Add glitter or sequins to the crown.
❷ Make the crown and face from 1 cup. Cut the crown spikes in the top.

The Lesson Connection ...
Joash, the boy king (2 Chronicles 22:10–24:16)
Make a puppet to represent Joash. Use it to tell his story.

Kings worship Jesus (Matthew 2:1–12)
Make king puppets. Draw arms holding gifts on the cups, or add paper arms to hold the gifts.

paper plate

Suncatcher

Directions ...
Choose a design from page 74 for a Bible story or theme, or design your own theme. Lightly trace the simple design on the back of the paper plate. Make the lines between pieces about ¼" wide. Cut out the sections, leaving the thick lines. Trace around the cutouts on tissue paper, about ¼" larger than the pieces. Cut and glue the tissue shapes around the holes on the back of the plate. As an option, write a Bible verse or phrase on the front of the plate. Punch a hole at the top and tie a piece of yarn or ribbon thru it for a hanger. Hang in a window.

Options and Variations ...
❶ Substitute a colored or foam plate.
❷ Substitute colored cellophane for tissue paper.

The Lesson Connection ...
Jesus gives us Holy Communion (Luke 22:7–20)
Trace the cup and bread pattern. Glue yellow tissue paper behind the cup and brown tissue paper behind the loaf. Write, "Do this in remembrance of Me" around the plate circle.

Pentecost (Acts 2:1–41)
Cut out 1 or several sections of a flame. Glue a red tissue-paper circle on the back of the plate. Write "I will pour out My Spirit" on the plate. Thank God for the gift of the Holy Spirit in your life.

Supplies ...
• Paper plate
• Pencil
• Scissors
• Colored tissue paper
• Glue stick
• Marker
• Paper punch
• Yarn or ribbon

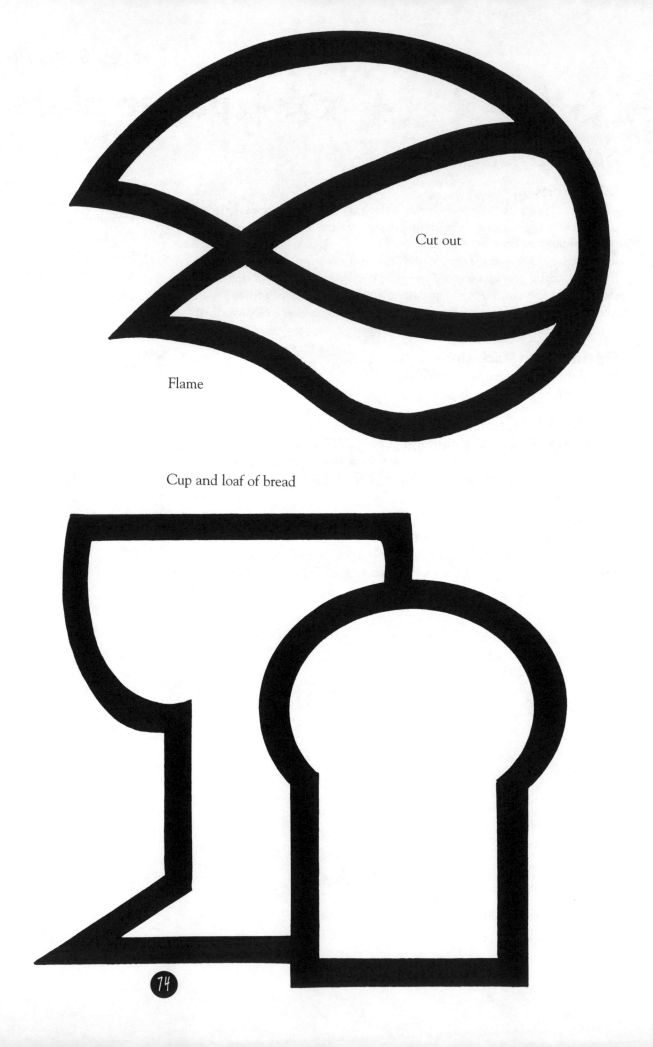

Cut out

Flame

Cup and loaf of bread

★★★★★★★★★★★**paper twist**

Bible Figure

Directions ...

Cut an 8″ length of skin-colored paper twist. Cut 3 10″ pieces of colored paper twist. Untwist the 8″ twist and place a cotton ball inside. Twist it back together to make a head and 2 arms. Untwist the 10″ pieces. Fold each in half and cut a small hole in the fold. Pull the pieces over the head piece, poking the arms out the sides. Cut yarn pieces to tie around the neck and center body as a belt. Cut short pieces of yarn, fray them, and glue on for hair and/or a beard. Add other details, as desired.

Options and Variations ...

❶ Insert a craft stick to make a stick puppet before tying off the puppet head. Poke the stick into a ball of oil-based clay to stand up the figure.

❷ Make a simple angel: Fold twist in half and put a cotton ball in the center. Twist a long metallic chenille wire around the cotton ball, then twist the wire ends together to make a halo. For wings, cut a 2nd piece of twist. Unfold it, twist in the center, and glue it to the back of the figure.

❸ Use figures in a diorama, or hang from a Christmas tree.

❹ Use paper twist instead of cornhusks and follow the directions found on page 20.

The Lesson Connection ...

Jacob's dream (Genesis 28:10–22)

Make an angel to set up in your room as a reminder of the protecting presence of these special messengers of God.

Witnesses for Jesus—Ascension (Acts 1:1–11)

Make a simple diorama of Jesus' ascension. Use white twist for Jesus' robe. Wrap a 2nd color over the shoulder; glue in place. Use brown yarn for hair and a beard. Glue the figure to the middle of a box lid covered with blue paper and cotton-ball clouds.

Supplies ...

• Colored paper twist
• Scissors
• Cotton ball
• Yarn
• Glue

Fold

photographs

Collage

Directions ...
Choose a shape or design as a backing for photographs. Cut out the people in the photos. Using the photograph size as a guide, draw the rest of the picture on the paper. Add details with paper or fabric pieces. To make the picture stand up, glue it to a piece of cardboard. Cut a right triangle of cardboard as tall as the backing. Fold over the tall edge and glue it to the backing.

Options and Variations ...
❶ Combine photographs with Bible figure drawings cut from lesson leaflets.
❷ Glue a cardboard tube to the back for a stand.
❸ Glue a paper clip to the back for hanging.

The Lesson Connection ...
Isaac is born (Genesis 21:1–7)
Cut a house shape from paper. Cut flaps for windows. Glue the paper to a cardboard backing. Glue photos of family members behind each flap. Write "Thank God for My Family" on the house.

Jesus blesses the children (Mark 10:13–16)
Make a class poster. Glue photograph faces onto poster board. Draw a body to go with each. Write the words "Jesus Loves (name)" on a heart placed in the hands of each person.

Supplies ...
• Photographs of people
• Paper
• Scissors
• Glue
• Markers or paint

plastic bottle ★★★★★★★★★★

Story in a Bottle

Supplies ...

- 2-liter plastic bottle
- Permanent markers
- Cardboard
- Scissors
- Construction paper
- Glue

Directions ...

Wash out the bottle and take off the label. Cut a hole in the side of the bottle. Cut a piece of cardboard for a base, about 1" bigger than the hole on all sides. Cut folded construction-paper shapes to illustrate a Bible story or theme, leaving a small flap on the bottom of each to glue the shape to the cardboard. Add other objects, as needed. Glue the bottle over the top of the cardboard base. Display the bottle on a table.

Options and Variations ...

❶ Add miniature figures or objects to the bottle.
❷ Construct objects from balsa wood, poster board, or other durable materials.

The Lesson Connection ...

God saves Noah and his family (Genesis 6:1–9:17)
Cut out an ark and rainbow, using the patterns on page 79. Add details with markers or crayons. Make a base 4–5" larger on all sides than the hole in the bottle. Glue the ark and rainbow in the center of the base. Glue the bottle over the base. Glue animal crackers on the base outside the bottle. Write "God Keeps His Promises" on the base.

God preserves Paul (Acts 27:1–28:10)
Draw water and a shoreline on a base. Use the patterns on page 79 to trace and cut out the sinking boat shape. Glue it in the water. Cut stand-up shapes for Paul, his friends, and the Roman soldiers. Add details with markers or crayons. Glue these to the shoreline.

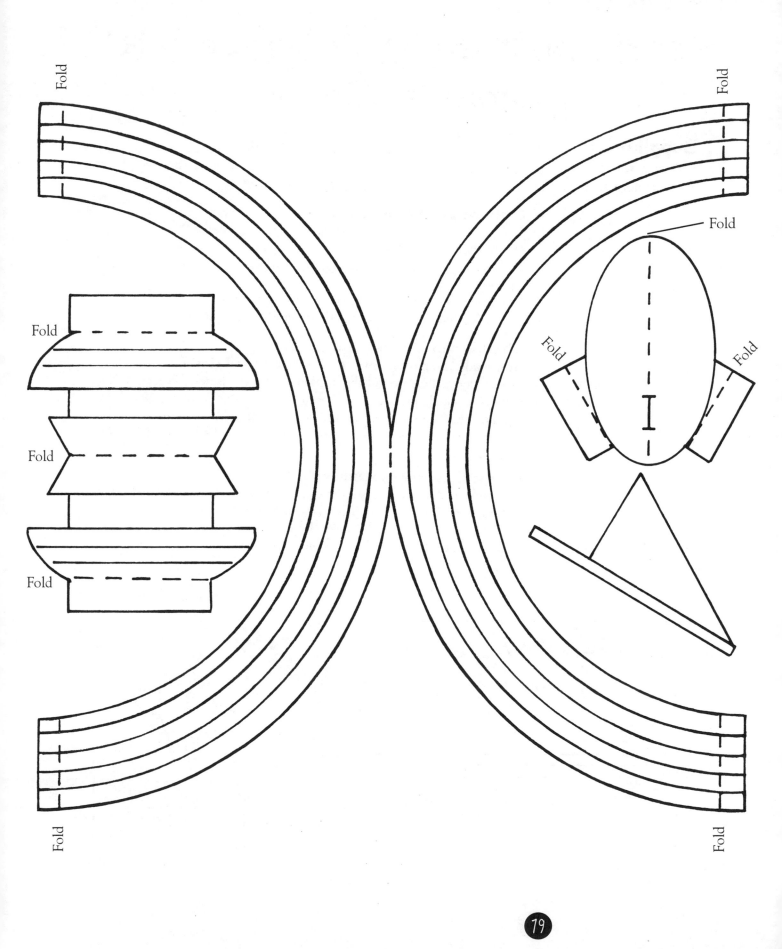

Fold

Fold

Fold

Fold

Fold

Fold

Fold

Fold

Fold

Fold

Fold

79

ages 5 and up

plastic bottle ★★★★★★★★★★

Story on a Bottle

Supplies ...
- Plastic bottle
- Permanent markers

Directions ...
Decide how to draw the story around the bottle. Consider showing only 1 part or the whole story. Rinse out the bottle and remove the label. Draw the story with permanent markers on the bottle.

Options and Variations ...
❶ Paint the design with acrylic paint or paint markers.
❷ Fill the bottle with colored water, sand, rice, or metallic strips.
❸ Place the bottle on its side and draw the action so it rolls with the bottle.
❹ Cut out the bottom of the bottle. Slip a picture to trace inside the bottle. Remove when finished. Or glue or tape drawings inside.

The Lesson Connection ...
God leads His people into the Promised Land (Joshua 3–4)
Draw a dotted line around the bottle to show the Israelites on their journey. Draw simple pictures to represent several things that happened to them on their desert journey. Add words, as needed. Fill with gravel, sand, or layered colored sand. (Color your own sand with powdered tempera paint.)

Jesus stills the storm (Matthew 8:23–27)
Draw a boat with the disciples in it. Draw waves around the bottle. Add water colored with blue food coloring and glitter. Glue the cap on with a hot glue gun (adults only). Shake the water to show the storm. Let the water settle to show how Jesus calmed the storm.

plastic canvas

Mobile

Directions ...
Cut shapes from plastic canvas and place on waxed paper. Fill the canvas with colored glue. Use different colors to make designs, if desired. Let dry. Cut and tie a different length of cord thru the top of each shape. Attach the shapes to a hanger.

Options and Variations ...
❶ Add sequins or colored plastic beads for decorations.
❷ Add glitter.

The Lesson Connection ...
God made the world (Genesis 1:1–2:3)
Design a favorite part of creation to put in a classroom creation mobile.

The good Samaritan (Luke 10:25–37)
Cut and decorate a heart shape. Make a cross in the center in a different color of glue. Tie a ribbon at the top. Hang it as a reminder that Jesus helps us love other people.

Pilate condemns Jesus (Luke 22:66–23:25)
Decorate a cross to help you remember that Jesus suffered, died, and rose again for you.

Supplies ...
- Plastic canvas
- Colored glue
- Scissors
- Waxed paper
- Cord

plastic canvas ★★★★★★★★

Ribbon Cross Medallion

Supplies ...

- Plastic canvas
- ¼" ribbon
- Scissors

Directions ...

Cut plastic canvas into a 4" square cross. Cut 3-row triangles at each end as shown. The inside row of each triangle should have 5 squares, the middle have 3 squares, and the outside have 1 square. Cut 2 40" pieces of ribbon. Leaving 6" of ribbon at the end, pull 1 ribbon from the bottom of the canvas thru the hole marked 1. Pull the ribbon across the top to the bottom right side, thru hole 2. Continue, going back and forth, following the number scheme and crossing the ribbon in the center, as shown. Do the same with the side arms, following the letters a–j to make the pattern. Finally, wrap each loose end of ribbon around the center and tie in the back. Cut another length of ribbon to necklace length and string the medallion on it.

Options and Variations ...

❶ Attach a metal pin clasp with a hot glue gun to the back of the cross. Wear the cross yourself, or give it as a gift.

❷ Tie lengths of ribbon to 1 end of the cross and use it as a Bible bookmark.

❸ Experiment with different kinds of ribbon and plastic-canvas colors.

The Lesson Connection ...

Jesus resurrects Jairus' daughter (Mark 5:21–24, 35–43)
Jesus showed love for Jairus and his wife by raising their daughter from the dead. He showed love for all people by dying on the cross and rising from the dead to give us new life in Him. Make a cross to wear to remember all God has done for us in Jesus.

Jesus rises from the dead—Easter (John 20:1–18)
The cross did not defeat Jesus. He rose from the dead. He is risen! He is risen indeed! Celebrate Easter by making this medallion in bright springtime colors to wear or to give to a special loved one.

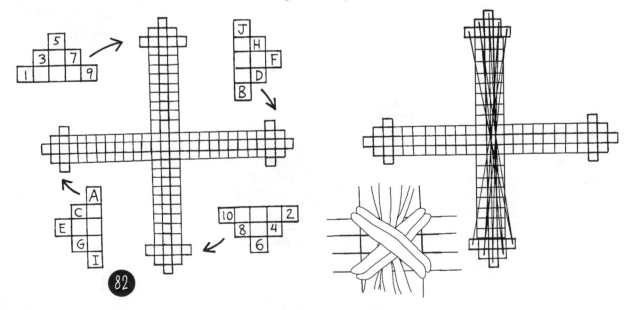

plastic lid

Ornament

Directions ...
Place the lid on the felt and trace around it. Punch a hole in the top of the lid and in the felt. Cut and glue the felt circle to the inside of the lid, matching the holes. Trace and cut a symbol from felt to glue to the center of the lid. (See page 84 for patterns.) Cut a ribbon and thread it thru the holes as a hanger.

Options and Variations ...
❶ Outline symbols with sequins or metallic fabric paint.
❷ Add your photograph to the center of the ornament.

The Lesson Connection ...
God calls Abraham (Genesis 12:1–3)
Cut a blue circle with a yellow star. Through Abraham's family, God gave a special baby, our Savior Jesus. Hang this and other symbols of the Savior from a special Advent tree to remember that God keeps His promises (to Abraham and to us).

John prepares the way for Jesus (Matthew 3:1–12; Luke 1:57–80)
Read these Bible verses together. Have the group brainstorm ideas to remind them of John the Baptist. Then have each person make an ornament. Hang these in a row in the classroom windows with a cross at 1 end to show that John prepared the way for Jesus. Ask people to tell what their shape tells about John.

Supplies ...
• Plastic lid
• Felt
• Pen
• Scissors
• Paper punch
• Tacky glue
• Ribbon

Angel

Manger

Person ("voice of one calling in the desert")

Shepherd staff

Star

Bee (wild honey)

Bell

Water drop

★★★★★★★★★★★ plastic wrap

"Stained-Glass" Picture

Directions ...
Cover table with newspaper. Cut pieces of cardboard and paper into the same size and shape for a design. Cut pieces of aluminum foil and plastic wrap about 2″ larger on all sides. Sketch a simple Bible picture or symbol on the paper. Tape plastic wrap over the paper and trace the picture onto it with a black permanent marker. Color with other markers, leaving spaces for the aluminum foil to show thru. Cover the cardboard with foil, then put the plastic wrap on top and tape the edges on the back. Attach a pop-top tab to the back as a hanger.

Options and Variations ...
❶ Skip the plastic wrap and color the foil.
❷ Draw the designs of stained-glass windows in your church.
❸ Use different colors of foil wrapping paper.

The Lesson Connection ...
David and Goliath (1 Samuel 17:1–58)
Cut a cardboard shield. Use "The Lord Is My Shield" in your design. Let this wall plaque remind you of God's protection.

The great catch of fish (John 21:1–14)
Make a "stained-glass" fish to remind you that God provides for all our needs.

Supplies ...
- Plastic wrap
- Aluminum foil
- Newspaper
- Paper
- Cardboard
- Pencil
- Scissors
- Masking tape
- Permanent markers
- Pop-top tab

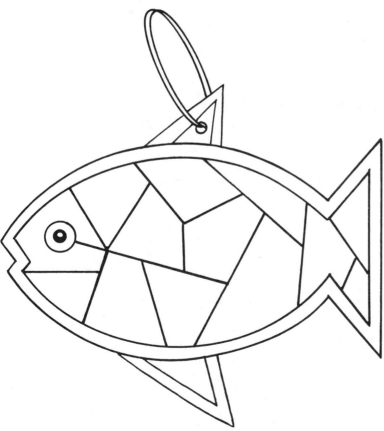

THE LORD IS MY SHIELD

poster board ★★★★★★★★★★★

Decorated Letter

Supplies ...

- Colored poster board
- Pencil
- Scissors
- Tacky glue
- Paper punch
- Yarn
- Markers or crayons
- Assorted lightweight objects

Directions ...

Outline the 1st letter of a person's name on poster board. Punch a hole at the top. Write a favorite Bible verse on 1 side. On the other, add drawings, stickers, lightweight objects, trim, buttons, paper cutouts, or other items appropriate to the lesson theme. As you work, talk about what the items say about the lesson theme. Tie a piece of yarn thru the hole to hang.

Options and Variations ...

❶ Punch holes around the letter and lace with yarn.
❷ Cut a letter for a Bible character and illustrate with pictures or drawings about his or her life.
❸ Hang a group of letters as a mobile.

The Lesson Connection ...

God made the world (Genesis 1:1–2:3)
Use an initial letter as a bulletin board for a course or school term. Write "God Made Me" on the letter. Add items of significance to it during the year.

Isaac is born (Genesis 21:1–7)
Cover numbers with birthday wrapping paper. Decorate each number with decorative stickers, ribbon, or curled ribbon to celebrate the students' birthdays. Say, "Each year of our life is a gift of the Lord."

God calls Isaiah (Isaiah 6:1–8)
Write, "God calls me by name. I am His" on the letter. Let students decorate with items that describe them.

Stephen witnesses about Jesus (Acts 6:1–8:1)
Cut out the letter *J* and illustrate it with pictures of Jesus' life. Use it to tell someone else the story of Jesus and His love for people.

pumpkin seeds

3-D Nature Collage

Directions ...

Wash and dry pumpkin seeds. Bake at 200°F for 25 minutes to kill insect eggs or larvae. Cut a cardboard circle. Lightly trace a simple pattern on the circle. Glue pumpkin seeds to the cardboard to make the desired pattern, adding other small seeds, if desired. Dry, then paint or leave a natural color. Glue a loop of metallic thread to the back as a hanger.

Options and Variations ...

❶ Add leaves made from painted cardboard or felt. Or fill cardboard leaf shapes with dyed pumpkin seeds.

❷ Make a sunflower: Glue birdseed or rice in the center. Add pumpkin seeds around it.

❸ Glue seeds to a plastic lid.

❹ Glue a seed flower to a wooden plaque. Add a Bible verse.

❺ Fill in other shapes with seeds (e.g., fish, cross).

❻ Spray with clear, acrylic sealer.

The Lesson Connection ...

Kings worship Jesus (Matthew 2:1–12)

Cut a star shape out of cardboard. Fill the star with seeds, starting in the center. When dry, do the same to the reverse side. Paint with metallic paint. Punch a hole at the top and tie thread thru for hanging.

God takes care of us (Matthew 6:25–34)

Cut a cardboard circle. Glue rice in the center and seeds around it to make a flower. Glue on a craft stick as a stem. Stick it into foam glued into the bottom of a flowerpot. Write "God helps me grow" on the pot with a permanent marker.

Supplies ...

- Pumpkin seeds
- Other small seeds (optional)
- Cardboard
- Tacky glue
- Scissors
- Acrylic paint
- Paintbrush
- Metallic thread

puzzle pieces ★★★★★★★★★★★★★★

Picture Frame

Supplies ...

- Puzzle pieces
- Cardboard
- Scissors
- Ruler
- Stapler
- ½" brad
- Glue
- Spray paint (optional)

Directions ...

To frame a 5" × 7" picture, cut 2 7" × 9" cardboard rectangles. Draw a box inside Piece 1, 1" from all edges. Cut out the inside, leaving a frame. Score a line on Piece 2 about 1" below the top. Trim ½" off the bottom edge. Cut a 1" × 2" cardboard tab and attach it to the bottom of Piece 2 with a brad. (This allows you to open the frame from the back to insert a picture). Cut a triangle. Score the edge and glue or staple it to Piece 2. Stand Piece 2 upright and adjust the triangle, if needed. Staple Piece 2 to Piece 1 along the top edge. Glue overlapping layers of puzzle pieces to Piece 1. Let dry, then spray paint, if desired.

Options and Variations ...

❶ Glue puzzle pieces around a cardboard, poster-board, or plastic circle to make a wreath. Write a Bible passage inside.

❷ Trace designs from Christmas cookie cutters and use these in place of the puzzle pieces.

The Lesson Connection ...

Jesus is born (Luke 2:1–20)
Cut a cardboard Christmas tree and glue green puzzle pieces on it. Write "Jesus" on it with a metallic paint pen. Attach a triangle to the back to make it stand up, or attach a cord to hang it.

Pentecost (Acts 2:1–41)
Glue white puzzle pieces to a dove shape.

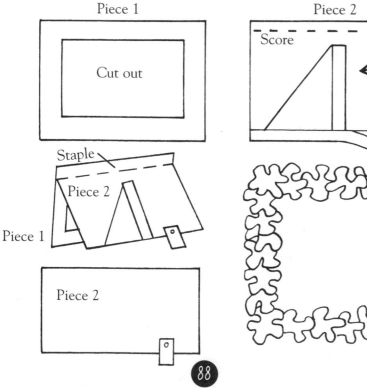

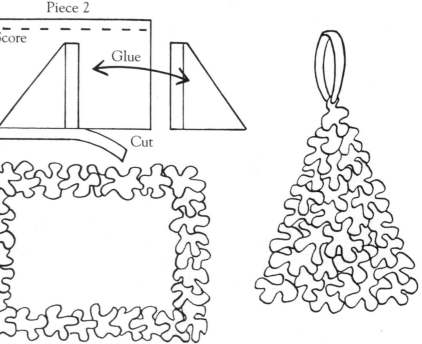

ribbon

Bird

Directions ...

(1) Cut 2 unequal ribbon strips. (2) Glue each together in a circle. (3) Glue the smaller circle (head) to the larger circle (body). (4) Fold paper. Cut a triangle on the fold and glue it to the head as a beak. (5) Cut a ribbon strip for wings. Cut a point at each end. (6) Glue it to the top of the body. (7) Cut a ribbon strip for the tail. Cut a notch at 1 end. Glue it onto the body. Glue the bird to a nest or twig, or fasten a string around it for hanging.

Options and Variations ...

❶ Add circles inside the large circle to add body fullness.
❷ Glue on a feather tail.
❸ Fringe the wing and tail ribbons.
❹ Wrap ribbon around a grapevine wreath. Add a bow to the top and a bird on the inside corner. Write a Bible verse on colored paper and glue it inside the center or on the side of the wreath.

The Lesson Connection ...

God made the world (Genesis 1:1–2:3)
Make different-colored birds to show the wonder of God's creation. Hang them together in a mobile.

John baptizes Jesus (Matthew 3:13–17)
Make a dove out of white ribbon to represent God's Holy Spirit coming down from heaven. Let it remind you that God's Spirit also came to you on your Baptism day.

Jesus dies for us (Mark 15)
Make a ribbon cross. Glue 4 ribbons of the same length together to make a cross. Glue 4 smaller, same-sized ribbons inside of them. Tie a thread hanger on the top.

Supplies ...

• Ribbon
• Scissors
• Paper
• Glue
• String

1   2   3   4

5   6   7a   7b   option

89

salt

Baked Clay Plaque

Supplies ...

- Salt
- Flour
- Water
- Mixing bowl
- Mixing spoon
- Rolling pin
- Plastic knife
- Drinking straw
- Cookie sheet
- Ribbon
- Sandpaper
- Watercolor paints
- Paintbrush and water

Directions ...

Mix dough: 1 part salt, 1 part water, 2 parts flour. Add more flour if too sticky or add more water if too dry. Knead 10 minutes, until soft and pliable. Roll out on lightly floured breadboard or waxed paper to ¼" thickness. Cut into shapes for a plaque. Score and wet edges, pressing down lightly to connect pieces. Imprint patterns or layer pieces to make your design. Make an indentation in the back to use for hanging, or make a hole in the top with a straw. Thread a ribbon thru the hole after baking. Bake on a cookie sheet at 250° until golden brown. Rub with sandpaper, then paint with watercolors.

Options and Variations ...

❶ Paint with tempera or acrylic paint.
❷ Spray with clear acrylic sealer for a more permanent finish.

The Lesson Connection ...

God saves Noah and his family (Genesis 6:1–9:17)
Cut a half-circle. Outline it with a coil. Add an ark shape in the middle. After baking, write "God Keeps His Promises" on the ark.

Jesus is the way to the Father (John 14:1–14)
Make an arrow plaque. Put clay letters for *Jesus* on the arrow. Punch a hole at the top for hanging.

salt

Self-Drying Clay

Directions ...
Mix 1 cup salt and ½ cup flour in a saucepan. Add food coloring to 1 cup of water, then add to dry ingredients. Heat on low temperature, stirring constantly until thick and rubbery. Cool. Add flour if too sticky, water if too dry. Store in airtight container.

Options and Variations ...
❶ Paint with a mixture of tempera paint, water, and white glue.
❷ Poke natural and artificial objects into dough. Let dry.

The Lesson Connection ...
God made the world (Genesis 1:1–2:3)
Make a collage by sticking nature objects into dough.

Elijah and the prophets of Baal (1 Kings 18:16–46)
Make gray dough with red, blue, and yellow food coloring. Roll into an altar shape. Poke pebbles into it. Place it on a flat round base with the words "The Lord Is God" written around it. Glue on tissue-paper flames.

Jesus stills the storm (Matthew 8:23–27)
Make a boat. Add a drinking-straw mast and paper sail. Write "Jesus Rescues" or a Bible verse on the sail. When dry, use your boat to act out the story.

The great catch of fish (John 21:1–14)
Make a fish plaque to remind you of this miracle. Push pasta pieces in it to make a cross or Jesus' name. Mount the fish on a Styrofoam tray.

Supplies ...
- Salt
- Flour
- Water
- Measuring cup
- Food coloring
- Pan
- Stove
- Spoon

THE LORD IS GOD

sand ★ ☆ ★ ☆ ★ ☆ ★ ☆ ★ ☆ ★ ☆ ★ ☆ ★ ☆ ★ ☆ ★ ☆ ★

Praise Paperweight

Supplies ...
- White sand
- Powdered tempera paint
- Cups
- Plastic spoons
- Plastic straw
- Baby food jars

Directions ...
Pour sand into cups. Mix powdered tempera paint with sand to color it. Spoon a little sand at a time into the jar, until full. Use a spoon tip or straw to vary the pattern on the side of the glass. Tighten lid. (Option: Glue the lid with a hot-glue gun.) Write a Bible verse or phrase around the glass jar with a permanent marker.

Options and Variations ...
❶ Mix wet tempera and sand. Allow several days to dry.
❷ Substitute salt for sand. Mix with crushed chalk for color.
❸ Substitute rice colored with food coloring. Spread in flat pan to dry.
❹ Paint the lid with spray or acrylic paint, or cover with paper, cardboard, or fabric.
❺ Attach a note to the neck of the jar with a ribbon.

The Lesson Connection ...
Jonah preaches in Ninevah (Jonah)
Draw a big fish with Jonah and bubbles on the jar. Layer natural sand on the bottom, with different colors of blue sand (with white as "highlight") on top. Shape waves into each layer. Write "God Heard Jonah's Prayer" on the lid.

Jesus gives sight to a man born blind (John 9)
Use bright colors inside the jar. Write words of praise to God around the side of the jar.

✫✫✫✫✫✫✫✫✫✫✫✫✫**sand**

Picture

Directions ...
Mix sand and tempera paint in cups to make a thin mixture that spreads easily. Lightly sketch a Bible story picture on a piece of cardboard, avoiding detail. Brush on the sand mixture, working from top to bottom. Apply with a plastic knife or spoon, if needed. Let dry. Shake off excess.

Options and Variations ...
❶ Add twigs, leaves, or other lightweight objects.
❷ Add flour to the mixture to make it easier to spread.
❸ Make a flour-and-water wash to use as contrasting paint.
❹ Rub off excess sand to make smooth areas on a dry picture.

The Lesson Connection ...
Moses and the burning bush (Exodus 3–4)
Outline a burning bush on a sandy background. Let your picture remind you that you too are called by God to serve Him.

God takes care of us (Matthew 6:25–34)
Outline simple bird and/or flower shapes. Fill in. Remember God's care for birds, flowers, and you.

Supplies ...
• Clean, dry sand
• Liquid tempera paint
• Cups
• Paintbrush
• Cardboard
• Pencil
• Plastic knife or spoon

ages 3 and up

soft-drink can ★★★★★★★★★★★★

Rhythm Shaker

Supplies ...
- Soft-drink can
- Dried beans
- Tape (wide)
- Paper
- Scissors
- Crayons or markers
- Glue

Directions ...
Have an adult carefully remove the pop-top tab. Rinse out the can and let dry. Spoon in beans. Use long strips of tape to close the drinking hole and lap over onto the sides. Cut paper to fit around the can. Decorate the paper with a Bible phrase or verse and pictures. Glue the paper around the can, covering the tape edges. Shake the can as you sing a familiar hymn of praise.

Options and Variations ...
❶ Cover the can with adhesive-backed paper, wrapping paper, wallpaper, or fabric.
❷ Add feathers, yarn, crepe-paper strips, or other decorations.
❸ Stamp a design on the paper.
❹ Add paper circles to the top and bottom of the can.

The Lesson Connection ...
David brings the ark to Jerusalem (1 Chronicles 15:25–29)
Write new words to a familiar tune to praise God. Write the words on the paper. Shake the can as you sing your song.

Jesus enters Jerusalem—Palm Sunday (Matthew 21:1–11)
Draw palm leaves and write "Hosanna" on the paper. Shake the can as you pretend to welcome Jesus into Jerusalem.

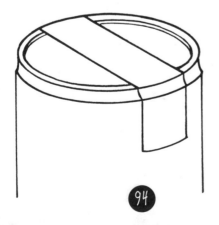

stickers

Game Cards

Directions ...
Measure and cut 2" × 4" pieces of poster board. Draw a line in the center and attach a sticker on each side. Play domino-like games, taking turns to match shapes.

Options and Variations ...
❶ Draw your own pictures or cut out identical magazine pictures.
❷ Use square pieces and make pieces to play matching games.

The Lesson Connection ...
God made the world (Genesis 1:1–2:3)
Make cards of plants and animals. As you match, say, "Thank God for (name of the object)."

God saves Noah and his family (Genesis 6:1–9:17)
Use stickers of different animals. Add paper cutouts of an ark and Noah and his family.

The great catch of fish (John 21:1–14)
Make game cards of fish. See if all the cards can be lined up or "caught."

Supplies ...
• Stickers
• Poster board or card stock
• Glue
• Scissors
• Ruler
• Pencil

ages 3 and up

straw ☆★☆★☆★☆★☆★☆★☆★★☆

Story Wreath

Supplies ...

- Straw
- Heavy-gauge wire
- Fine floral wire
- Wire cutters
- Adhesive Velcro squares
- Decorative materials

Directions ...

Have an adult cut a piece of heavy-gauge wire and shape it in a circle. Hold straw against the circle and wrap fine-gauge wire around it at 2" intervals. Attach Velcro squares to the wreath and to the back of decorative items.

Options and Variations ...

❶ Make a vine wreath: Curve 4–6 fresh vines around a wire circle. Soak older vines in warm water until soft. Wrap 1–2 vines around the circle to hold the other vines together.

❷ Write words on a wooden circle or heart, glue to a ribbon and hang from the center of the wreath.

The Lesson Connection ...

God saves Noah and his family (Genesis 6:1–9:17)

As you tell the story, let the children add Noah's family and animals to the wreath. Hang a rainbow from the center.

Jesus is born (Luke 2:1–20)

Let the children attach nativity characters as you tell the story of Jesus is born. Hang a star from the center.

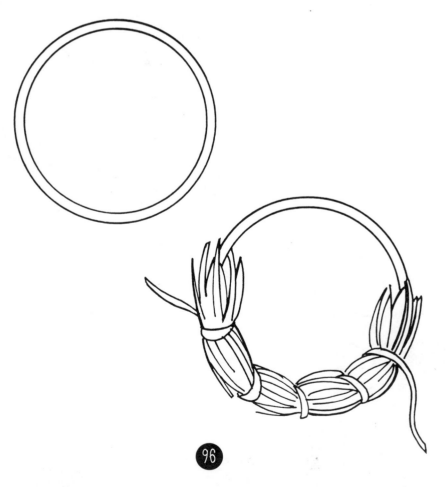

★★★★★★★★★styrofoam tray

Ornament

Directions ...
Stamp a Styrofoam tray with a cookie cutter. Cut out imprint. Poke a hole in the top with a pen point. Tie a thread thru for hanging.

Options and Variations ...
❶ Decorate with glue and glitter.
❷ Glue on fabric pieces, trim, and sequins.
❸ Decorate with textured fabric paint.
❹ Punch designs in the Styrofoam with a pen point.

The Lesson Connection ...
Jesus is born (Luke 2:1–20)
Use Christmas cookie cutters to make shapes. Glue on glitter and sequins. Use the ornaments to decorate a tree in your room.

Healing a man born lame (Acts 3)
Cut out 2 or more heart shapes. Cut and glue on fabric squares for a quilt-like effect. Hang the hearts on the wall to remember God's love for you. Ask Him to help you love others.

Supplies ...
• Styrofoam tray
• Cookie cutter
• Scissors
• Thread
• Pen point

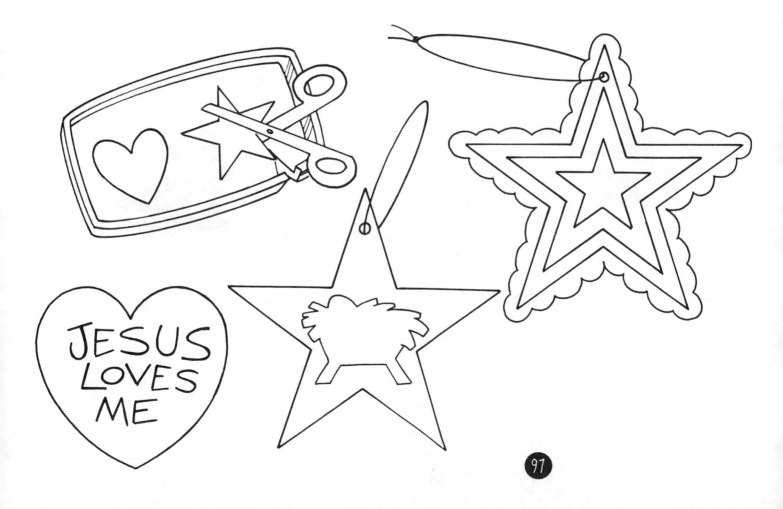

tempera paint ★★★★★★★★★★★

Silhouette Painting

Supplies ...

- Liquid tempera paint
- Lamp
- Paper
- Masking tape
- Pencil
- Paintbrush
- Wallpaper
- Glue

Directions ...

Tape paper on a wall. Shine the lamp at the paper. Stand a person between the paper and lamp. Outline the shadow of the person's face on the paper. Take down the paper. Paint the profile. Cut a wallpaper square as a frame. Cut out the profile and glue it to the wallpaper. (For younger children, cut out the profile, then let them paint it.)

Options and Variations ...

❶ Glue profile to a framing mat. Add a Bible passage.
❷ Make a classroom mural of several silhouettes.
❸ Trace and cut profiles from aluminum foil.

The Lesson Connection ...

Isaac is born (Genesis 21:1–7)
Isaac was a special gift to his parents. Each child is a precious gift from God. Celebrate the unique way God has made each person by making silhouettes.

Jesus, light of the world (John 8:12)
Jesus lights the way to a new, forgiven life. Let the light in this craft show the new you (profile) to the world.

JESUS LOVES B.J.

★★★★★★★★★★★ tissue paper

Sharing Flower

Directions ...
Fold tissue paper lengthwise. Cut scallops along the unfolded edge. Thread a needle and loosely stitch about an inch from the fold. Gather the paper along the thread to form a circular flower. Write a Bible word or phrase on the plate (e.g., "Grow in God's Word"), then glue it inside the petals. As you do so, talk about what you can do to help make these Bible words grow in your hearts during the week. Give the flower to someone else to share God's love with them.

Options and Variations ...
❶ Make a sunflower: Cut leaves from yellow paper. Glue sunflower seeds to the center.
❷ Use different sizes and colors of paper plates for the center or cut a paper circle.
❸ Layer different colors of tissue paper for petals.

The Lesson Connection ...
God hears Hannah's prayer (1 Samuel 1:1–2:11)
Talk about how mothers, like Hannah, pray for and help children. Make a gift flower for the children to give to their moms to say thank you. Write a thank-you note on the center.

The parable of the sower (Matthew 13:1–23)
Write "Grow in God's Word" on the center. Hang the flower as a reminder to grow in God's Word thru daily Bible reading.

Jesus resurrects Jairus' daughter (Mark 5:21–24, 35–43)
Write a Bible verse that stresses God's power to help in times of need (Psalm 50:15). Give the flower to someone who is sick.

Supplies ...
• Tissue paper sheets
• Scissors
• Needle and thread
• Tacky glue
• Small paper plate
• Marker

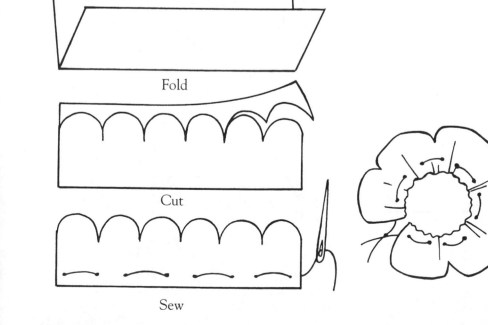

Fold

Cut

Sew

GROW IN GOD'S WORD

wallpaper scraps ★★★★★★★★

Patchwork Cross

Supplies ...

- Wallpaper scraps
- Poster board
- Pencil
- Ruler
- Scissors
- Glue
- Paper clip

Directions ...

Cut a 7″ poster-board square. Lightly pencil a 2″ grid with a ½″ border on the poster board. Cut and glue on 2″ wallpaper squares to make a pattern. Cut and glue ½″ X 7″ rectangles around the edges as a frame. Glue a paper clip to the back of the "quilt" for hanging.

Options and Variations ...

❶ Use fabric, wrapping paper, or plastic adhesive squares.
❷ Check quilt pattern books for more complicated patterns to fit a Bible story or theme (e.g., butterflies, stars, or hearts).
❸ Cut some squares into triangles for more pattern variety.
❹ For younger children, outline shapes on the poster board.
❺ Write a Bible verse or phrase around the frame.
❻ Glue squares together to make a class project.

The Lesson Connection ...

Jesus dies for us (Mark 15)
Make a cross. Use 9″ squares for smaller children. Encourage older children to develop more intricate patterns.

Jesus rises from the dead—Easter (Mark 16:1–8)
Cut an Easter butterfly to glue in the center of a square. Cut and glue shapes around the edges.

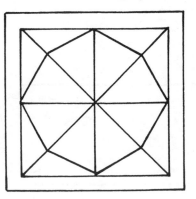

washcloth

Puppet

Directions ...
Cut a 5″ piece of yarn. Place the washcloth flat in front of you. Roll the right and left sides to the center. Fold down about ⅓ of the washcloth, 1 roll behind the other. Tie the yarn around the folded-down top to make a neck. Pull out the sides from the folded-over part to make arms. Insert and glue a craft stick inside to make a puppet. Glue on movable eyes.

Options and Variations ...
❶ Add details with yarn, felt, or fabric.
❷ Omit the craft stick. Instead, fold the washcloth over a 6″ piece of yarn or cord. Tie it thru the top fold for a hanging puppet or ornament.
❸ To make an angel: Fold a washcloth in half, twist the middle of a metallic chenille wire around it to make the head, then twist the ends to make a halo.

The Lesson Connection ...
God cares for Jacob (Genesis 28:10–33:20)
Use different puppets to tell the story of Jacob and his family.

An angel rescues Peter (Acts 12:1–19)
Make washcloth puppets for Peter and the angel. Use them to tell the story.

Supplies ...
• Washcloth
• Yarn
• Scissors
• Craft stick
• Craft glue
• Movable eyes (optional)

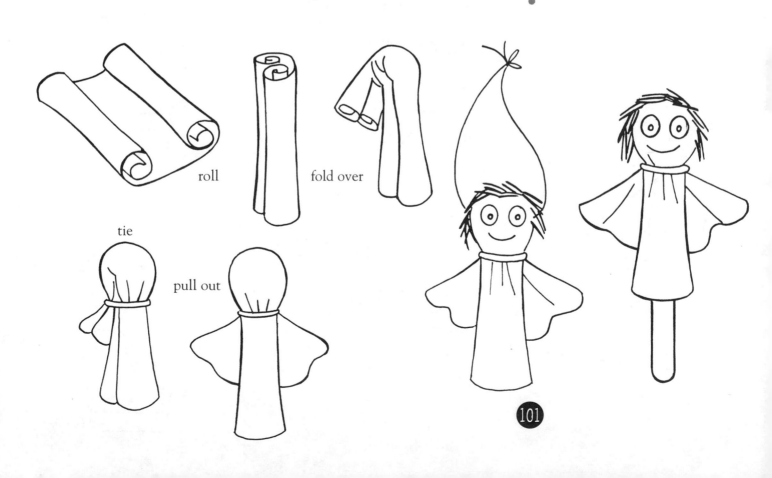

roll   fold over

tie

pull out

waxed paper ★★★★★★★★★★★

Suncatcher

Supplies ...
- Waxed paper
- Scissors
- Pencil
- Colored tissue paper
- White glue
- Water
- Bowl
- Paintbrush
- Paper punch
- Yarn

Directions ...
Cut waxed paper twice the length you want your finished suncatcher. Fold in half. Unfold. Lightly sketch a design on the waxed paper. Cut out tissue-paper shapes to match your design. Lay them on the inside bottom half of the waxed paper until you have a design you like. Then remove them. Mix 1 part glue to 2 parts water and paint the inside bottom half of the waxed paper. Stick the tissue-paper shapes carefully on the waxed paper because they will tear if moved. Paint glue on the inside top half of the waxed paper. Fold the top of the waxed paper down onto the bottom. Let dry a day. Cut into a shape, if desired. Punch a hole at the top and tie a piece of yarn thru it for hanging.

Options and Variations ...
❶ Glue pressed leaves, flowers, ribbon, decorative paper, yarn, glitter, netting, fabric, or colored cellophane inside the waxed paper.
❷ Use acrylic varnish instead of white glue.

The Lesson Connection ...
God gives His people food and water (Exodus 16:1–17:7)
Use different colors of paper to make favorite foods God has given you. Cut and hang from a clothes hanger to make a mobile .

Jesus rises from the dead—Easter (Luke 24:1–12; Matthew 28:1–10; 1 Corinthians 15:1–11)
Fill in a cross outline with brightly colored tissue paper. Add glitter, ribbon, sequins, and other decorative trim.

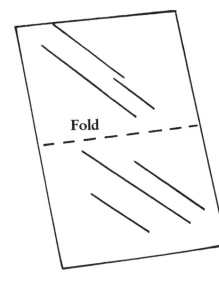

Fold

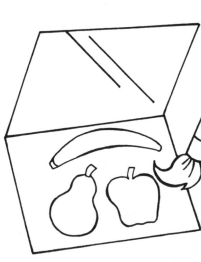

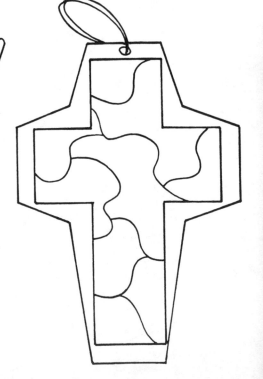

wire

Wall Decoration

Directions ...
Pick a cookie cutter to copy. Cut wire about 3″ longer than the cookie cutter circumference. Leave about 1½″ on the end, then shape the wire around the cookie cutter, starting at the top. Twist the wire ends together. Loop another piece of wire around the twist. Tie a ribbon around the top for hanging.

Options and Variations ...
❶ Leave longer ends and use as a bubble wand for classroom celebrations.
❷ Attach the wire as a wreath decoration.

The Lesson Connection ...
A widow helps Elijah (1 Kings 17:7–16)
Do not twist the wire ends; poke them into a large cinnamon stick. Tie a bow around the top of the stick. Write a word or phrase on the stick with a permanent marker. Use as a wall hanging, reminding you to find ways, like the widow, to help others in need, whatever your circumstances.

Jesus accepts a Samaritan woman (John 4:1–42)
Use a gingerbread man cookie cutter to outline a figure of Jesus with His accepting arms open wide. Make a robe by ignoring the leg lines. Add extra wire pieces to make a sash across the chest. Bend wire into a large heart and attach the figure to it. Add a ribbon at the bottom of the heart.

Supplies ...
• Bell wire (available at hardware stores)
• Scissors
• Cookie cutter
• Ribbon

wooden figure ☆★☆★☆★☆★☆★☆★☆★☆

Puppet

Supplies ...
- Wooden craft figure
- Fine-tipped markers
- Fabric and/or yarn

Directions ...
Draw a face and clothes on the wooden craft figure. Make different sizes and characterizations. Add fabric clothes or wind yarn around the figures to make clothes. Use the figure to tell or review a Bible story.

Options and Variations ...
❶ Adapt other small wooden shapes for props: small wooden vases can be used as water jars.
❷ Draw a tabletop stage on paper. Move the figures on it as you tell a story.
❸ Substitute cut dowel pieces for wooden craft shapes. (Use dowels with larger diameters for younger children because of a choking danger.)

The Lesson Connection ...
God heals Naaman (2 Kings 5:1–19)
Draw the road Naaman took to get from his home to Israel on paper. If you wish, trace a map outline. Make puppets for the servant girl, Naaman, his wife, and the prophet Elisha. Move the figures as you tell the story; let children move them to retell it.

Jesus is born (Luke 2:1–20)
Make a box stable for the puppets. Have children take turns making and setting up the characters. To make the manger, cut a small tube in half and glue the pieces back-to-back. Fill the manger with excelsior. Add a small wooden figure wrapped in a fabric blanket as baby Jesus.

wooden spoon

Kitchen Decoration

Directions ...
Choose a Bible picture and draw or paint it on the spoon. As an option, have an adult spray acrylic sealer over the painted spoon. Have an adult use a hot glue gun to attach a paper clip to the back for hanging.

Options and Variations ...
❶ Tie a piece of raffia, ribbon, cord, or yarn around the spoon. Hang up the spoon with the tie.
❷ Place several decorated spoons in a container.
❸ Decorate spoon handles with nontoxic markers or craft paint. Use when cooking.

The Lesson Connection ...
God blesses Ruth (Ruth)
Write "God Bless You" on a wooden spoon. Draw wheat heads to each side. Draw wheat stalks down the handle of the spoon. Tie with raffia. When you give it to someone as a kitchen decoration, express the hope that God bless the recipient as He did Ruth.

Jesus feeds 5,000 (Luke 9:10–17)
Draw a favorite food inside the spoon. Write "God Gives Me Food" around it. Tie a bow around the spoon and hang it up in the kitchen as a reminder that all your food comes from God.

Supplies ...
• Wooden spoon
• Acrylic paint or markers
• Paintbrush
• Acrylic sealer (optional, for **adult use only**)
• Paper clip
• Hot glue gun **(adults only)**

wrapping paper ★★★★★★★★★★

Bible-Verse Stationery

Supplies ...
- Wrapping paper (new or used)
- Plain cards and envelopes
- Fine-point markers
- Rubber cement

Directions ...
Pick wrapping paper with a design to match a Bible passage. Consider seasonal (Christmas or Easter paper) or nature patterns. Cut out a picture or design for the front of a card. Glue it on. Write a favorite Bible verse on the inside of your card. Cut out another small picture and glue to the envelope flap. Share God's love with others by giving them the card you have made.

Options and Variations ...
❶ Cut designs from fabric or wallpaper. Outline shapes with a glitter pen, metallic marker, or fabric paint.
❷ For younger children, duplicate a seasonal message to glue inside. Let them write their own names.
❸ Glue or tie a ribbon bow to the card.

The Lesson Connection ...
God made the world (Genesis 1:1–2:3)
Cut out animal and plant shapes. Write a thank-you note to someone who inspires your creativity.

God saves Noah and his family (Genesis 6:1–9:17)
Cut a rainbow shape from multicolored wrapping paper. Add the words "God Keeps His Promises."

Jesus rises from the dead—Easter (Luke 24:1–12; Matthew 28:1–10; 1 Corinthians 15:1–11)
Make Easter or sympathy cards with designs cut from Easter wrapping paper.

Sending the disciples (Matthew 28:18–20)
Combine shapes and Bible passages to make witness messages.

Jesus is born (Luke 2:1–20)
Cut designs from Christmas wrapping paper to make a Christmas note card. Or use designs from birthday wrapping paper to emphasize Jesus' birthday.

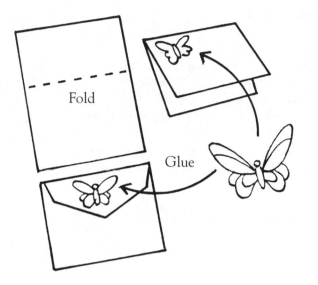

Fold

Glue

GOD LOVES YOU.
Love, anna

HE LIVES!

yarn ⭐⭐⭐⭐⭐⭐⭐⭐⭐⭐⭐⭐⭐

Bible Figure

Supplies ...

- Yarn scraps
- Drinking straw
- Scissors
- Craft glue

Directions ...

Cut a straw into 5 pieces—2 long, 1 medium, and 2 short (*fig. 1*). Glue the long straws to either side of the medium straw (*fig. 2*), leaving part of the medium straw sticking out for a head. Wrap yarn on the figure from the top to the bottom (*fig. 3*). Glue down the yarn ends. Wrap both short pieces (arms) with yarn, leaving 1 end unwrapped for hands (*fig. 4*). Glue the arms to either side of the body under the shoulders (*fig. 5*). Wrap yarn around the top of the arms several times to secure them. Glue down yarn ends. Wrap yarn around the top of the medium straw to make a head. Glue to the body (*fig. 6*), and glue down yarn ends. Add frayed yarn for hair and/or a beard.

Options and Variations ...

❶ Wrap craft sticks or clothespins.
❷ Wrap embroidery floss around toothpicks for smaller figures.
❸ Add fabric scraps for details.
❹ Make hanging decorations, bookmarks, or storytelling puppets.

The Lesson Connection ...

Jesus promises to always be with us (Matthew 28:16–20)
Make a figure of Jesus. Wrap the body with white yarn. Glue down red or brown yarn for a tunic. Use for storytelling, or add yarn for a Bible bookmark.

An angel visits Mary (Luke 1:26–55)
Make 2 figures, 1 for Mary and 1 for the angel. Use blue yarn for Mary and white for the angel. Loop several pieces of yarn together and tie in the middle for angel wings (*fig. 7*). Make other characters from the Christmas story to hang on a tree.

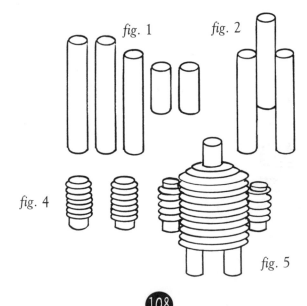

fig. 1   *fig. 2*   *fig. 3*

fig. 4   *fig. 5*

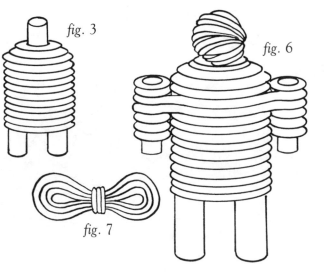

fig. 6

fig. 7

ziplock bag

"Stained-Glass" Window

Directions ...

Cut paper to fit inside the ziplock bag. Sketch a Bible picture or symbol on the paper. Outline with a dark crayon and fill in the design with other colors. Dab cooking oil on a paper towel and lightly rub over the crayon picture. Wipe off excess oil. Put the picture inside the bag and zip it. Punch a hole in the top of the bag and string yarn thru to hang in a window.

Options and Variations ...

❶ Punch holes around the whole perimeter of the plastic bag. String yarn thru the holes and tie a bow at the top.

❷ Use colored pencils instead of crayons.

The Lesson Connection ...

A widow helps Elijah (1 Kings 17:7–16)

Make bubble-shaped letters to spell "Trust in the Lord." Fill the letter centers with bright colors. Use the decoration as a reminder to trust God to take care of all your needs.

Jesus teaches us to pray (Matthew 6:5–15)

Cut paper in a window shape. Outline praying hands in the center and add stained-glass shapes around them.

Supplies ...

• Plastic ziplock bag (any size)
• Paper
• Scissors
• Pencil
• Crayons
• Cooking oil
• Paper towel
• Paper punch
• Yarn

A Bible Story Index ★☆★☆★☆★☆